BARRY FUNNY

"Despite years of medication, Dave Barry is still the funniest damn writer in the whole country. Let's hope he never grows up."

—Carl Hiaasen

"I'm so pleased to have received an advance copy of Dave's book and use most of the material myself. He is truly the funniest man living in the three-mile 'safe' zone off the shores of America."

—Steve Martin

"Dave Barry's best book so far, which is saying a lot. We in the print media are seeing our world collapse around us. There aren't enough newspapers left to line the bottom of a canary cage. Magazines are thinner than my hair. And 'writing' is done only on Wii. But here's Dave Barry, flourishing like never before, with a book that's funnier than ever, greeted with clamorous demand by eager hordes of fans. Let's kill him."

—P. J. O'Rourke

I'll Mature
When I'm Dead

Dave Barry's Amazing Tales of Adulthood

Dave Barry

G. P. Putnam's Sons
New York

PUTNAM

G. P. PUTNAM'S SONS
Publishers Since 1838
An imprint of Penguin Random House LLC
375 Hudson Street
New York, New York 10014

The essay "Colonoscopy" originally appeared in the *Miami Herald,* in somewhat different form.

The author gratefully acknowledges permission to quote e-mail text and use "Shark Photograph" by Sandy L. Goodrich
"Sphere" image 2007 © Pedro Tavares. Image from BigStockPhoto.com
"DNA" image 2007 © Pawel Szczesny. Image from BigStockPhoto.com

The Library of Congress has catalogued the G. P. Putnam's Sons hardcover edition as follows:

Barry, Dave.
I'll mature when I'm dead : Dave Barry's amazing tales of adulthood / Dave Barry.
   p.   cm.
   ISBN 978-0-399-15650-2
   1. American wit and humor.   I. Title.
   PN6162.B2975   2010   2009052665
   814'.54—dc22

First G. P. Putnam's Sons hardcover edition / May 2010
First Berkley trade paperback edition / April 2011
First G. P. Putnam's Sons trade paperback edition / September 2017
G. P. Putnam's Sons trade paperback ISBN: 9780425238981

Printed in the United States of America
13 15 17 19 20 18 16 14

Cover photograph of the author copyright © 2010 by Bill Wax/Daniel Portnoy
Cover design by Nellys Li

This book is dedicated to everybody who buys this book.
Without you, I would have to get an actual job.

Contents

I'll Mature When I'm Dead

Introduction

When a man reaches a certain point in his life, he feels a need to pass along the wisdom he has gained to younger generations. Of course the younger generations pay no attention; they're busy tweeting podcast YouTube blog apps on Facebook, or whatever the hell they're doing these days.

But if the Internet ever goes down and the younger generations have some spare time, I hope they read this book. It's a group of essays I wrote, mostly based on the theme of what it means to be an adult.

"Hah!" you are saying. "What would YOU know about being an adult?"

That's a fair point. In my long career (1887–2005) as a newspaper columnist, I was not known for being the voice of maturity. I was known for being the voice of discussing what would happen if a cow exploded on a commercial airplane flight.[1]

But since I stopped writing my weekly column, some things have changed. For one thing, there was a serious economic recession. Was this because the nation was devastated by the loss of my column? Modesty prevents me from speculating. But, duh.

For another thing, I've had time to reflect. A lot of people think that all I do in retirement is sit around watching TV, drinking beer, and passing gas. My wife thinks this, for example. But when I appear to be an inert sack of flatulent flesh on the couch, I am in fact reflecting, at least during commercials.

And when I'm not reflecting, I've been having significant life experiences. In the past few years I watched my son get married; watched my daughter play many soccer matches and perform in ballet recitals lasting longer than the Spanish-American War; got a dog named Lucy; rode in a fire truck with Clarabelle the famous Walt Disney cow;[2] had some medical adventures involving direct medical assaults on some of my most personal regions; took up spinning; ran for president; nearly won the Nobel Peace Prize; and spent the equivalent of the gross national product of Uruguay on veterinarian fees in an effort to repair a persistent injury to Lucy's tail caused by the fact that she wags too hard.

These life experiences, plus my reflections, were the inspira-

1. Bad things.
2. Fortunately she did not explode.

tion for the essays in this book. With one exception, they have never been published in a newspaper. They're longer than my weekly columns were, because I wasn't limited by rigid newspaper length limits (currently seventeen words per column, unless they are big words such as "refrigerator"). This meant that, in writing this book, I was able to "stretch" artistically—to go beyond simply writing a few booger jokes on a given topic, and instead write literally *dozens* of booger jokes on a given topic. Yes, it was a lot of effort, but if these essays help you in some way—by teaching you something useful about relationships, or parenting, or just getting through this crazy thing we call adulthood—then I for one will be surprised.

Throughout this book, I have tried to be as honest and accurate as possible, except when I am lying. I take full responsibility for everything you are about to read; any misstatements or errors of fact are solely the fault of global climate change. In conclusion, I hope you enjoy this book, and if you come away from reading it with just one message, let it be this: If a veterinarian suggests that you can somehow keep your dog from wagging its tail, that veterinarian is smoking crack.

The Elephant and the Dandelion

~~~~~~~~~~

(A Defense of Men)

My wife has a friend whom I will call Bernice. (That is not her real name. It is not anybody's real name.)

Bernice is an attractive, smart, funny, middle-aged single woman who would love to be in a committed relationship with a man. My wife knows approximately 1,700 attractive, smart, funny, middle-aged single women who would love to be in a committed relationship with a man. (I don't mean with the *same* man.) (Although at this point they might not rule it out.)

Several times a week, after talking with one of these women, my wife delivers a rant (it runs about seventy-five minutes, including a bathroom break) about how WRONG it is that there are all these attractive, smart, funny, middle-aged single women out there, and they CAN'T FIND A MAN. My wife has a theory about why this is, namely: Men are idiots.

My wife believes that men tend to have insanely high physical standards regarding the kind of woman they're willing to settle for. She notes that a middle-aged man can have tarantula-grade nose hair, b.o. that can cause migrating geese to change course, and enough spare tissue to form a whole new middle-aged man, but this man can still believe that he is physically qualified to date Scarlett Johansson.

"What's *wrong* with these men?" my wife asks purely rhetorically. "Don't they have *mirrors?*"

It is true that men can appear to be superficial about what qualities they seek in the opposite sex, as shown in this scientific chart:

What Women Look for in Men	What Men Look for in Women
Intelligence, kindness, a sense of humor, a stable career, loyalty, honesty, integrity, reliability, a willingness to share the load of parenting and housework, good hygiene, and a reasonable level of physical attractiveness.	Gazombas.

But does this mean that men are nothing but a bunch of shallow low-life sex-obsessed horn dogs? Yes. But men have a solid scientific excuse: biology.

As we know from attending high school, the human body is

actually made up of trillions of tiny one-celled animals called "cells," which clot together to form important organs such as the spleen, the jowls, and the goiter. Every single human cell contains "DNA," which is a special molecule that your body leaves behind at crime scenes so the police can identify you. But DNA has another important purpose: It contains your "genetic code," which enables you to pass along to future generations your distinguishing characteristics, such as hair color, age, hating the Yankees, etc. There are two crucial facts you need to know about DNA. The first one is:

Your DNA is in charge.

You may think *you* are in charge, but you are not. Your relationship to your body is the same as the relationship between a coach and a soccer team of four-year-olds. The coach can shout all the instructions he wants about kicking the ball, but if the players prefer to stand around picking their noses, they will stand around picking their noses. Likewise, your body does not do what you want; it does what your DNA wants. This leads us to crucial DNA fact number two:

The only thing your DNA thinks about is reproducing itself.

Your DNA wants to put its imprint on the entire human race, like the Nike Corporation. This goal is shared by both male and female DNA molecules, but they achieve it in very different ways. To understand the difference, let's take a look at actual photographs of two DNA samples. The first was taken from a woman:

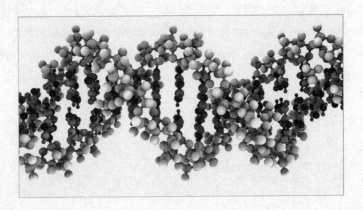

This one was taken from a man:

If we look closely, we can see subtle differences between these molecules, the main one being that the female DNA is more complex. The reason is that in order for female DNA to reproduce, the female it occupies—this is crucial—*has to have a baby.* And even if she starts really early and is a total slut, *she can only have a limited number of babies.* And even after she has a baby, if she wants her DNA line to continue, *she has to nurture that baby* until it can survive on its own, which with modern human babies does not happen until they are in their mid-thirties.

So for human females, reproduction is a very complicated and drawn-out process. It can take her weeks just to find an acceptable maternity bathing suit. Then there's all the paraphernalia she must buy for the baby—the stroller that costs as much as, but is more technologically advanced than, a Toyota Celica; the adorable little teensy baby shoes; the cute designer baby outfits that the baby will fill with poop.

Now a rational person, by which I mean a man, might ask whether the baby really *needs* all these things, especially the shoes, since the only thing babies do with their feet, once they discover them, is cram them as far as possible into their mouths.

But a rational person is not making these decisions. The woman's DNA is, and it is taking no chances. For whatever chemical reason, it is convinced that the baby needs cute little shoes, so the baby WILL have cute little shoes, just as the baby's room WILL have wallpaper festooned with cute little baby animals. If you try to stop a severely pregnant woman from providing these things for her baby, she will crush your skull with a Diaper Genie. This is not personal. She's obeying her DNA, which is doing what it believes it has to do to nurture her child—or, more accurately, her child's DNA.

As the child grows older, the woman continues to engage in behavior that may seem irrational to a normal person. A good example is birthday parties. These are considered by most women to be a vital part of child-nurturing, which is why every year, when my daughter's birthday comes around, my wife becomes—and I say this with the deepest affection—a dangerous lunatic.

I'm not saying our daughter shouldn't have a birthday party. I'm just saying I could organize one in an hour. I'd order some pizzas, get a cake at the supermarket, organize some fun party games for little girls—"Run Around Shrieking," "Run Around Shrieking Some More," etc.—and boom, there's your party. I'm not saying it would be the greatest birthday celebration ever. For one thing, it would be roughly a month after my daughter's actual birthday, because I am not good with dates. But it would get the job done.

My wife, on the other hand, believes the party should be along the lines of the Super Bowl halftime show, but more elaborate. Her birthday parties always have themes. One year the theme was *The Wizard of Oz*, and among the props she found on the Internet (including a piñata shaped like a ruby slipper) was a "yellow brick road," which consisted of a roll of extremely slick yellow plastic, which she instructed me to unroll on our front walk. It was raining, so I pointed out, in a very reasonable tone, that if we put slippery plastic on the already-slippery sidewalk, people could get hurt.

Did you ever see the movie *Species*, in which what appeared to be an attractive woman was actually a camouflaged alien reptile creature who could kill a man by sticking her hideous reptile tongue into his mouth so far that it came out through the back of his skull? When that creature was about to strike, it had *exactly* the same facial expression as the one on my wife when I suggested that maybe we should not put out the yellow brick road. Her view was: Yes, people might get injured, perhaps even killed, but the theme of the party is *The Wizard of Oz*, and *by God we are going to have a yellow brick road.* And so of course we did.

The nurturing instinct is not limited to children. It causes women to engage in a wide range of other behaviors that men find unnatural, including:

- Giving gifts and/or thoughtful cards for virtually every occasion including the onset of daylight saving time;
- Thinking about relationships;
- Talking;
- Not really caring about offensive rebounds;
- Worrying;
- Buying scented candles the size of fire hydrants.

The list goes on and on and on. A typical woman's brain is swarming, night and day, with vague feelings of guilt caused by the nagging worry that somebody, somewhere in her vast complex network of family and friends *needs more nurturing.* That's why she's in a bad mood.

Men are a whole different biological story. A man can't have babies, of course, so the only way his DNA can reproduce itself is if he gets a woman pregnant. The thing is, the man's DNA's odds improve if, while the first woman is off buying tiny unnecessary shoes for her future offspring, he gets *another* woman pregnant. In fact—and remember this is the DNA thinking, *not* the man—*the more women the man gets pregnant, the better the odds that his DNA will survive.* He is genetically programmed to attempt to mate with pretty much any available woman or reasonably soft object, then move quickly along.

So to summarize: A woman is designed like a female elephant, with a long gestation period followed by years of mothering; whereas a man is designed more along the lines of a dandelion, which randomly spews large numbers of seeds all over the place, then pretty much forgets about them. Neither the elephant nor the dandelion is "right." They're both perpetuating their DNA, but they're biologically designed to use very different strategies, which is why you so rarely see a meaningful, long-term, mutually fulfilling relationship between an elephant and a dandelion.

This brings us back to Bernice. Remember? My wife's attractive, middle-aged single friend who would love to be in a committed relationship with a man? We'll use her as our example of why it's pretty much hopeless. Bernice is, like my wife, a sportswriter. A while back they were at a major sporting event, and Bernice revealed to the other women sportswriters that in several days she was going to go on a blind date for lunch. So the other women sportswriters wished her luck and went back to work.

Ha-ha! Of course that is not what happened. What happened was, the Women's Emergency Relationship Support Network signal went off—*BWOOP! BWOOP! BWOOP!*—and the other women sportswriters immediately ceased sportswriting so they could devote their full analytical and reportorial and Googling skills to the many questions raised by the impending date. Some concerned the man: Exactly who was he? How old? What did he do? What were his prior relationships? Was he cute? Did he have any unmarried friends? Were *they* cute?

Then there were the questions for Bernice, the critical one being: What should she wear? Team Bernice settled on a skirt, but then there was the issue of length. It couldn't be too short, because then Bernice would appear to be trying too hard. But it couldn't be too long, because then she would appear to be a nun.

After much discussion, coaching, and preparation, Bernice was finally ready to go on her date. But she didn't really go alone. She was accompanied, in spirit, by my wife and the rest of the team of women sportswriters. In a way, Bernice was accompanied by all the other women who have ever existed, surrounding her in an invisible scented cloud of supportive womanity, rooting for her to find a suitable mate and settle down and replicate and nurture her DNA.

Now consider the guy. Let's call him The Dandelion. I don't know him, but I guarantee he did not have a team of guys behind him. And I doubt he did much preparing. Probably fifteen minutes before the lunch his BlackBerry beeped, and he thought: "Whoa! I have a date!" Then he tried to remember if he was wearing the underwear without the ketchup stains.

When Bernice and The Dandelion met for lunch, they did not have the same goals. Bernice may have *told* herself that it was just lunch, but on some level, she was evaluating The Dandelion's suitability as a lifetime partner featuring reliability, loyalty, kindness, etc. Whereas The Dandelion, not to put too fine a point on it, was evaluating her gazombas, and probably the gazombas of every other woman in the restaurant.

Go ahead, call him a pig. But remember that without male pigs, there would be nobody to mate with female pigs, at least outside of West Virginia. My point is that The Dandelion, like Bernice, was simply doing what he was genetically programmed to do.

Naturally the date didn't work out. It's amazing that *any* date involving a human male and a human female *ever* works out. Whatever way the human race came into existence—whether it was through divine creation, or intelligent design, or Darwinian evolution—crack was definitely involved. Our DNA is the Windows Vista of genetic code: The design is faulty, and it doesn't seem fair to be constantly blaming only one gender for this. Remember that millions of us men manage to overcome our DNA, get married, settle down, and live happily ever after with our wives and never even *think* about mating with another woman such as—to pick a name at random—Scarlett Johansson.

But getting back to Bernice, and all the other women who've had trouble finding a man: Is there any hope for them? Of course there is! If you're one of these women, remember this: There are literally billions of men on the planet, and the statistical probability is extremely high that one of these men is exactly the right guy for you. So if you're patient, and you keep a positive mental attitude, and you don't give up hope, the odds are very good that you will never meet this guy, because he probably lives in some place like Uzbekistan. So you might want to consider Plan B, which is becoming a nun, assuming you're OK with the longer skirt.

If You Will Just Shut Up, I Can Explain

A Man Answers Questions from Women

Recently, I started spinning with my wife.

No, you pervert; spinning is a kind of exercise. You go into an enclosed space with other people and mount stationary bicycles and pedal furiously to oldies music until the atmosphere is 93 percent b.o. fumes and you feel as if shrews are gnawing your lungs, but you cannot stop because a spinning instructor with mutant pedaling powers is hectoring you to *pedal faster* until the end of the song, after which ANOTHER song starts and you must pedal *more*. This is when you discover how long certain songs really are. "Paradise by the Dashboard Light," for example, is longer than dental school.

I am the only man in the spinning class. The rest of the spinners are women, including the instructor, a terrifyingly fit personal trainer named Erica, who could defeat you in hand-to-hand combat using only her earlobes. If we ever decide to get serious about forcing captured terrorists to talk, she is the person to do it.

> **ERICA (STARTING SONG):** Now we're going to pedal to *this*.
> **TERRORIST:** Not "American Pie"! Please! Waterboard me!

Anyway, when the spinning class is over, the women often talk, and as you might expect, the topic they discuss most often is the technical features of their cell phones.

Seriously, their favorite topic is relationships, defined as: What Is Wrong with Men. I have been a man for my entire adult life, and I have spent much time in male-only groups, and I can state for a fact that women think men are a lot more interesting, as a conversation topic, than men think women are. Sure, men will talk about women, but generally these conversations are brief and factual:

> **FIRST MAN:** Did you see that?
> **SECOND MAN:** Yeah.
> **FIRST MAN:** Whoa.
> **SECOND MAN:** Yeah.
> **FIRST MAN:** So how do you like your new phone?

Sometimes, if a man is in a relationship and he's talking with a really close male friend, the conversation will get a little deeper:

FIRST MAN: Tracey's really pissed off at me.

SECOND MAN: Why?

FIRST MAN: I don't know.

SECOND MAN: That sucks.

FIRST MAN: Yeah.

SECOND MAN: So how do you like your new phone?

But this kind of probing, soul-baring discussion about women is rare for men. Whereas women, including women who hardly know each other, can talk for hours about men without getting bored. They find us fascinating and mysterious. They want to understand us. This is baffling, because men are not complicated and generally state their views clearly when asked, especially if you compare them to women.

Take gifts. If you ask a mother what she wants for Mother's Day, she'll say, "Oh, you don't have to get me anything." This is of course a lie, as most men have learned, usually painfully. If you were stupid enough to actually give this woman nothing for Mother's Day, she would be deeply hurt. Because when she says you don't have to give her anything, what she means is that she doesn't want to have to *tell* you to give her something; she wants you to spontaneously, on your own, without prodding, select some thoughtful and appropriate and utterly useless gift that shows how much you appreciate her and how much you think about her on Mother's Day. She wants a *fuss*.

Whereas when a man says he doesn't want anything for

Father's Day, he means—pay close attention—that *he doesn't want anything for Father's Day.* He has already received too many Father's Day gifts that he will never use. He views Father's Day as a load of crap dumped upon men by the restaurant and greeting-card industries, working in collaboration with women. He would be thrilled if his family celebrated Father's Day by going to a restaurant without him, leaving him on the sofa, snoring to the soothing sounds of televised professional golf.

But when men say they don't want anything for Father's Day, women choose not to believe them. Women *love* Father's Day, because it involves cards and gifts and family get-togethers and various other fuss-tivities that men generally dislike and women generally love. This is the real reason why we celebrate Father's Day, not to mention birthdays and anniversaries, which men would not even pretend to care about if women did not make them.

(I realize I am making some very broad generalizations here. Deal with it.)

Another example is weddings. When two young people become engaged, the bride-to-be always tells the groom-to-be that she really truly wants him to be an equal partner in the wedding planning, because the wedding is for *both* of them, not just her. This is of course another lie. What she means is that she wants him to agree enthusiastically with the wedding plans she will make in collaboration with her mom, her friends, her wedding planner, her caterer, her florist, and her 4,538-page, seventeen-pound issue of *Modern Bride*. If the groom-to-be's views were actually considered, the wedding would be a far more relaxed affair, possibly involving go-carts. Or it might not happen at all, since many grooms-to-be, when they see their fiancée mutate into a cross between Martha Stewart and George Patton, begin to wonder if it might be a good idea to just put the whole thing on ice for a decade or two.

Not that anyone asks them.

My point is that we men are not mysterious; there is no need for women to find us baffling. In hopes of ending this confusion, I recently conducted a survey of women whom I selected on the scientific basis of being either (1) friends of my wife, or (2) on the Internet. I asked these women to submit the questions that bothered them most about men. I got many, many responses, the gist of which is neatly summarized by my wife's friend Amy, who asked: "Do men realize how unfathomably stupid women think they are; and, if so, why don't they do anything about it?"

Note that this question has a somewhat negative tone. This was typical. Not one woman asked a question that implied men might have any positive qualities. They did not ask: "How can men be so darned rational all the time?" Or: "What can men teach women about somehow managing to get through life with fewer than sixty pairs of shoes?"

Anyway, my hope is that, by giving simple, straightforward answers to these women's questions using the Q and A format, I can clear up some of the misunderstandings women have about men. I'll begin with a question that many of the women asked, a question that seems to trouble women in general more than the danger of an Earth-asteroid collision:

Q. *Why don't men put the toilet seat back down after they pee?*
A. Because they care. Human males are descended from prehistoric tribal warriors who had to defend the women and children in their tribe from vicious savage enemy tribes who could attack at any time without warning to rape and pillage and plunder. So these early males had to be constantly vigilant. They had to pee standing up with their heads on a swivel. They could not afford to waste precious seconds aiming the pee stream or putting down the toilet seat, because the enemy might choose just that moment of distraction to strike and perform acts of vicious savage plundering on the women and children. That was a risk these brave and courageous and manly warriors of long ago were simply unwilling to take. This same protective instinct is still deeply ingrained in men today, not that we expect any thanks.

Q. *But prehistoric tribes didn't even HAVE toilet seats!*
A. Exactly.

Q. *Why don't men listen when we talk? When we want to share our feelings with you, to talk about things that are important*

to BOTH of us—our children, our careers, our relation-
ships; or when we simply share the details of a trying day, to
get a little sympathy—why is it that you barely even bother
to hide your lack of interest? How can you care more about
some sports event on TV, or some unimportant message on
your cell phone, than the feelings of the person who cares
most about you, and is always blah blah blah? Why is it al-
ways our responsibility to worry about blah and blah, not to
mention blah, while you are unable to spend even two min-
utes thinking about blah? Blah blah blah blah blah. Hello?
Did you hear anything I just said?

A. What?

Q. WHY DON'T MEN LISTEN TO WOMEN?

A. They do listen. But they listen for specific information.
Men are problem-solvers. They are doers. When you
talk to them, they are listening to determine (a) what
the problem is, and (b) what they need to do about it,
so that they can (c) resume watching ESPN. When they
have the information they need, they stop listening.

In the early phases of your relationship with a man,
he listens to you a lot, because he is trying to solve a very
important problem, namely, getting you to have sex
with him. No matter what you talk about—your work,
your friends, the fruit flies of the Ryukyu Islands—the
man will pay close attention, because you might give

him a clue indicating how he can get you to become naked.

Once he has solved this problem, he becomes more selective in his listening. He will be most alert when you talk about a specific, clearly defined problem, because he can then use his reasoning skills to come up with a solution. For example, if you tell him that the car motor is making a funny noise, he will listen intently, then determine what he needs to do, namely, wait for a few days, in case it goes away.

But when it comes to feelings, the man is in trouble. Scientists using brain probes have determined that the average man has approximately one feeling per hour, versus 850 for the average woman. So the man is not as comfortable with feelings as you are. When you pour out your feelings to him, he tries to figure out what the specific problem is so he can take action. But he quickly becomes confused, because there doesn't seem to *be* a problem; he doesn't understand what you want him to *do*. If you tell him you don't want him to do anything, that you just want him to listen to you and to share *his* feelings in return, you only make it worse, because at any given moment he has just the one feeling, and it's usually something along the lines of "My balls itch."

Eventually the man concludes that for some reason

you periodically have a massive internal buildup of feelings that must be released in the direction of another human being. He adopts a strategy of monitoring these releases for key words or phrases indicating a problem that he might have to do something about, such as "fire," "internal bleeding," or "district attorney." Otherwise he's just hunkered down, waiting for the feelingstorm to blow over, maybe sneaking a peek at the sports highlights so his time is not completely wasted.

Q. *But doesn't it occur to men that, because these feelings are important to somebody he cares about, they should also be important to HIM?*
A. What?

Q. *Never mind. Why do men feel that they must know what's on every TV channel all the time?*
A. Back in prehistoric times, when men had to protect their loved ones by peeing standing up, they also were responsible for feeding their families by hunting. This meant they had to be constantly scanning the environment, always searching for prey.

Q. *So you're saying that when men change channels, they're looking for prey?*
A. No, breasts.

Q. *Why ARE men so obsessed with breasts?*

A. In many species, males and females use visual cues to attract each other for the purpose of facilitating reproduction, which is necessary to avoid extinction. For example, the male peacock drags around an enormous tail, which he displays to the female peacock, who responds: "Whoa! That is some large tail you have! Let's engage in reproductive activity in the form of getting it on!"

Yes, she is treating the male as a sex object. But this does not bother him. He does not think, "Why is she so obsessed with my tail? It's just *feathers*, for God's sake. She can't even make eye contact with me!" Why doesn't he think this? Because his brain is the size of a Cheerio. But also because he knows that unless the female becomes attracted to him, there will be no reproduction, and if there is no reproduction, then peacocks will become extinct. So he is *happy* to display this important visual cue to the opposite gender.

Q. *Are you suggesting that women should go around displaying their breasts to males?*

A. I was talking about peacocks. But hey, sure.

Q. *Why do men refuse to read instructions?*

A. As we have established, men have a lot on their plate, what with protecting their loved ones, preventing the extinction of humanity, etc. When a man purchases a necessary appliance such as a TV with a flat screen the size of a squash court, he cannot afford to fritter away valuable minutes reading the owner's manual, especially when the first seventeen pages consist of statements like: WARNING: **Do not test the electrical socket by sticking your tongue into it.**

A man does not need instructions written by and for idiots. A man already knows, based on extensive experience in the field of being male, that the way to handle an appliance is to plug all the plugs into the holes that look to be about the right size or color, then turn everything on and see what happens. This is the system I use, and it has proved to be 100 percent effective roughly 65 percent of the time.

Granted, sometimes I have to make some adjustments. Two years ago I got a high-definition TV, and after I set it up, my wife (a woman) complained that the picture did not look like high definition to *her*. So I made some adjustments in the form of explaining patiently to her that she was incorrect, because it was a high-definition TV, and therefore, by definition, the picture she was seeing on it was in high definition.

For months, every time my wife watched television, she told me that the picture didn't look like high definition to her, and I had no choice but to roll my eyes in a masculine fashion to indicate that she was getting in over her technological head. Then, after we'd had the TV for about a year, she decided—you know how women get these crazy ideas—to look at the manual. She removed the plastic sealing and began reading, and on page 28, somewhere after the warning about not using the TV as a life raft, she found a section about "inputs," and she changed something, and there was a dramatic improvement in the quality of the picture. I argued that this could be coincidence—that maybe at that exact moment, the TV networks had decided to change from high definition to even *higher* definition. But my wife was sure it was because of what she had read in the manual. She even tried to show *me* the manual, but of course I did not look directly at it, because of the danger that my penis would fall off.

Q. *Is that also why men refuse to ask directions?*

A. If Man A asks Man B for directions, Man B, realizing that Man A is a weak, direction-asking type of male who probably also reads owner's manuals, could decide to attack Man A's village and plunder his women. Man A is not about to run that kind of risk. But there is more to it than that. Men are explorers. They do not follow the herd. If "everyone" says that the best way to get to a certain mall is to take a certain road because that is the road that the mall is located on, a man wonders if there might be another, better, as-yet-undiscovered route to that same mall. If Columbus, back in 1492, had taken directions from the so-called "experts" about how to get to India, he would never have set out in the opposite direction across the Atlantic Ocean, and today there would be no such thing as Microsoft, Dairy Queen, or syphilis.

Q. *So are you basically saying that all of the things that women perceive as flaws in men are actually virtues, without which the human race would today be facing widespread misery, destruction, death, and possibly even extinction?*
A. Also, no Dairy Queen.

Q. *I never realized any of this. Now I feel so guilty for all the time that we women have spent thoughtlessly carping about men. I feel terrible about our insensitivity, and all the pain we must have caused you. I feel . . . Excuse me, are you listening?*
A. What?

The Heart of Dadness

A Letter to a First-Time-Father-to-Be

S o you're about to become a dad! That is wonderful news. As the poet Wordsworth once said, "Fatherhood is truly the most . . . HEY! You kids put down those hatchets RIGHT NOW!"

The poet Wordsworth's point was that, although fatherhood is a rewarding experience, it's an experience that you will sometimes wish was rewarding somebody else. Nevertheless, if you ask any dad if fatherhood is worth it, he will immediately answer yes. Why? Because his wife might be listening.

No, seriously, he will answer yes because fatherhood is a great thing, for reasons I will attempt without success to explain later. But you need to be prepared for some big changes in your lifestyle.

To begin with, for a while after the birth of your child you will have the same sex life as a waffle iron. This is understandable, considering the physics of childbirth. Imagine that you have spent seventeen straight hours trying to push a mature grapefruit the entire length of your urinary tract, and you have a rough idea of what your wife goes through when she has a baby. You will be as welcome in her private region as German troops are in Paris. She may sleep with a Taser. But rest assured that, in time, she will come around. And by "in time" I mean, "in a really long time."

The other side of that coin is that for a while you might not feel quite as attracted to your wife as you used to. For one thing, she'll have gained some weight, and she'll tend to dress in "post-maternity" fashions purchased from The House of Tarps. For another thing, milk will be squirting out of her breasts. This is perfectly natural; when you think about it, this is the actual reason why your wife has breasts in the first place. But it's still going to seem weird to you, because like most men, you have always viewed breasts as fun recreational items existing purely for your personal enjoyment. Now all of a sudden they're producing dairy products! It's as if a tennis racket suddenly started dispensing ketchup.

Very Important: During this sensitive postpartum time, you must be very careful not to say anything negative about your wife's appearance. On the other hand, you must not say anything *positive* about your wife's appearance, because she'll know you're lying. And whatever you do, do NOT give her the impression that you're deliberately *avoiding* talking about her appearance. This might be a good time to enlist in the navy.

I'm just kidding, of course.[1] You'll want to stick around so that you can experience the first amazing weeks of parenthood, a magical adventure during which you will discover many wonderful things, such as what is on TV at 3:46 A.M. You've probably heard that newborn babies sleep an average of sixteen hours per day. What you may not have heard is that, rather than do all of their sleeping in one big chunk, babies divide the day into roughly two hundred seven-minute naps. This means they wake up roughly two hundred times a day, and they always wake up cranky.

So as new parents, you will spend the first few months, day and night—especially night—doing virtually nothing except trying to de-crankify your baby. This is where it is critically important that you and your wife function as a team. Your role on the team, when the baby cries, is to say to your wife, in a loving and supportive team-player tone: "I would get up and feed the baby myself, but unfortunately I do not have milk squirting from my nipples." Try not to resume openly snoring until your wife has left the bedroom.

If feeding doesn't work, or if your wife, needing a little personal time, has burst out of the house and is sprinting off down the street in her nightgown, screaming, it's your turn to try to quiet the baby. Here's what you do:

---

1. Not really.

1. Go to the baby's crib and locate the baby's head and the baby's butt. In a standard baby, the head will be crying, and the butt will be leaking.

2. Slide one hand under the baby's head and the other under the baby's butt, then gently lift the baby to your shoulder. If you're holding the baby correctly, there should now be vomit on your shoulder. If there is poop on your shoulder, you are holding the baby upside down.

3. When you have the baby oriented correctly, walk around in a circle while jiggling the baby and singing, in a gentle, soothing voice, this traditional lullaby:

Hush little baby, don't say a word
Papa's gonna buy you a mockingbird
And if that mockingbird don't sing
Papa's gonna put it in the food processor

This lullaby will help relieve some of the tension you're feeling as you—only recently a normal person, now a sleep-deprived zombie staggering around in circles while a tiny human barfs on you—begin to truly understand how much your lifestyle is going to change.

I distinctly remember when this really sunk in for me. It was 1980, and I, a brand-new father, was at some friends' house during a New Year's Eve party. The party was going on downstairs;

I was upstairs with my two-month-old son, Robert, who was lying in the exact center of our hosts' bed, taking one of his two hundred daily naps. I was watching him, in case he woke up crying, or suddenly figured out how to play with matches.

From downstairs I could hear the roar of the party. It was a major party, the kind of party where some of the guests could very well wake up naked in a foreign country. A little before midnight I took a quick peek downstairs, and I saw that the party had reached Gator Stage. This is the point a party reaches when certain guys, having consumed perhaps eight or nine more shots of tequila than they really need, find that two things are true:

1. They wish to dance.
2. They cannot stand up.

The solution is for these guys to dance in a style known as "the gator," which is when you lie on the dance floor and writhe around to the music in what you believe to be a rhythmical manner. You run the risk that the vertical dancers will step on you, but if you're truly in gator mode, you wouldn't notice if a UPS truck parked on your head.

So there I was, peeking down at my friends having crazy fun—fun that, the previous New Year's Eve, I had been part of. I went back and sat on the bed with Robert, and it hit me: Not only was I not going to be gatoring this New Year's Eve, but *I was never going to gator again.* Dads don't gator. Oh, you might attend a party where gatoring has commenced, and you might even consider joining in. But as you start to get down on the floor, some part of your brain—the Dad Lobe—will kick in and remind you that you need to relieve the babysitter. And you will step over your friends (or on them; it doesn't matter) and head for the door.

So you will not be partying as hard. Here are some other things that will change:

> When you're part of a group of guys who are arguing about whether it's possible to jump from a given roof or balcony into a given swimming pool, and the group finally decides that the only way to settle it is to have one guy actually attempt it, you will find that you no longer volunteer to be that guy.
>
> You will also set off fewer fireworks than you used to, and virtually none indoors.
>
> You will learn to do everything with one arm, because the other arm will be holding the baby. You *will*, at some point, go to the bathroom while holding the baby.
>
> You will have frequent daytime fantasies—elaborately detailed, very explicit fantasies—about napping.
>
> You will reach the point where you will, in the same perfunctory manner that you now check your text messages, pull back your baby's diaper and peer down to determine

the status of the Poop Zone. You will be able to do this in a restaurant while chewing your entrée.

You will exchange your sporty fun car for a practical seventeen-cupholder vehicle with a name like the Nissan Capacity, the interior of which, over the next five years, will gradually become coated with a quarter-inch-thick layer of a substance consisting of Cheerios, Juicy Juice, and spit.

Over the next five years, you will spend roughly forty-five minutes, total, listening to songs you like, and roughly 127,000 hours listening to songs exploring topics such as how the horn on the bus goes.[2]

You will attend far fewer movies with plots involving sex and violence, and far more movies with plots involving talking raccoons trying to find the Magic Pine Cone.

Am I saying that, once you become a dad, you're never going to have fun again? Yes.

Wait, I mean no. You can still have fun; you will just have to make some adjustments. For example: One Thanksgiving I was at a gathering of families at the home of Gene Weingarten and Arlene Reidy. It was traditional at this gathering for the men to help the women prepare the food. We did this by leaving them alone and going outside to play a game of touch football in the

_____

2. It goes "Beep! Beep! Beep!"

backyard, from which Gene, the thoughtful host, had removed approximately 60 percent of the dog turds.

One of the regulars in this game was a guy I'll call Bob.[3] This particular year, Bob had a problem: His wife, whom I will call Mary,[4] had asked him to watch their infant daughter, which meant he was stuck on the sideline holding the baby in one hand and a beer in the other.

And then, at what is known in sports as a Critical Juncture, one of the players on my team had to leave the game. We looked at Joel.[5] Now, as a dad, he had to make a decision, weighing various factors. On one hand, he was responsible for his infant child, a precious, irreplaceable human life, utterly helpless and totally dependent on him. On the other hand, *it was third down.*

"You can*not* tell Mary," he said, setting his daughter down on the lawn. (He also—and this is a measure of how seriously a man takes a third-down situation—set down his beer.) We huddled and came up with a play, diagramming it so that none of the pass routes went too close to the baby, because that is the kind of responsible adults we are. I don't remember what actually happened in the play. All I remember is that it was crucial.

The point is that Joel was able to fulfill his parental responsibilities *and* have carefree guy fun for a stretch of nearly forty seconds. I realize this doesn't sound like much compared with,

3. Joel Achenbach.
4. Because that is her name.
5. Whoops.

say, a weekend in Vegas. But as a dad, you will learn to take what fun you can get.

What's more, in time you'll discover—and here we are getting to the Message—that the fun you're missing out on is more than made up for by something new—something you've never known before; something wonderful.

It will happen when your baby is around three months old. He or she will be lying on his or her back, making random baby movements and sounds, as though communicating with invisible space aliens. Suddenly you and your baby will make eye contact, and something will pass between you. Then you will lean over, and—as millions of fathers have before you—you will place your mouth on your baby's belly and blow in such a manner as to make a sound like a musk ox breaking wind. This will have a profound effect on your baby. This will strike your baby as the funniest thing that he or she has experienced in his or her entire life. Your baby will laugh, and it will be the purest and best laugh you ever heard. You will laugh, too, and you will have no choice but to re-flatulate the baby's belly, and your baby will think it's even funnier the second time. So you'll do it again, and again, and again, and it will get funnier *every time*. You and your baby will be laughing and drooling like a pair of morons. Which you are, but in a good way.

You will then begin to understand something that is at the very heart of Dadness: Although your wife is probably a better natural parent than you are when it comes to things like remembering to feed and clothe and provide medical care for the baby, you also bring some important items to the parental table, with Exhibit A being fart jokes. As a guy of the male gender, you are genetically programmed to have superior skills in this area. You will find that you're also better at, among other things, animal noises, peekaboo, scary stories, hide-and-seek, blocks, water balloons, and anything that involves batteries. Your child will gradually discover your talents in these areas, and he or she will become your biggest fan. In those magical early years, you will be, to your child, the coolest person on the planet, with the possible exception of the Wiggles.[6] The two of you will form a bond—a permanent, unbreakable bond that will connect the two of you, powerfully and forever, until your child reaches age eleven and realizes that you're a dork.

But you'll get through that when the time comes. The point is, something is going to happen between you and your baby, and it will be like nothing that ever happened to you before, which is why nobody, least of all me, can even begin to explain to you why it's so great. But it is; just wait. The longer you live, the more clearly you'll see that no matter what else you've accomplished in life, the best thing you ever did, simple as it sounds, was be a dad.

And someday, decades from now, when your kids have all grown up and moved out, you and your wife (if you're lucky

---

6. You'll find out.

enough to still be together) will turn to each other and think back to how the two of you set out, totally clueless, on this amazing adventure. You'll shake your heads, and you'll smile. You might even kiss.

And then, if you're *really* lucky, she'll put down her Taser.

Dance Recital

Here's a simple and fun experiment:

Select, at random, a man who has one or more daughters. Place a gun to this man's head and tell him he must do one of two things:

1. Have his prostate examined by a scorpion.
2. Attend a dance recital.

He's going scorpion. Yes, he knows it will be unpleasant. But he also knows that eventually it will end. This is not necessarily true of the dance recital.

I speak as a father who has attended three major recitals, each of which, for all I know, is still going on. Don't get me wrong: I love to watch my daughter dance. I'm just not crazy about watching the entire daughter population of North America dance. But you have no choice, under the recital system as practiced in my neck of the woods. Here's how it works:

Every week, for many weeks, you take your daughter to the dance studio, which is a building in a strip mall almost entirely obscured by a giant cloud of estrogen. There your daughter learns, step by step, two dance routines, selected from the major dance genres: Ballet, Tap, Jazz, Hip-Hop, Modernistic, and Weird.

Your daughter will perform her two routines at the recital, so she has to practice them at home. This means that she—and therefore you—must listen to the same two songs over and over and over and over and over and over and over and over and over and over and over, to the point where, even if you liked the songs originally, you start fantasizing about getting a time machine and going back into the past and whacking the composers. You might also take Hitler out while you were back there in the past, but your highest priority would definitely be the composers.

Finally the day of the recital arrives. The morning is entirely taken up with preparation, which is very stressful for everybody involved, by which I mean your wife. There's a lot to do. For one thing, there are the costumes. Your daughter must wear a different costume for each routine, because God forbid she should appear onstage twice with the same costume. So for each routine, you are required to buy a costume, which your daughter will never ever wear again, because that is the system used by the dance-recital-costume industry, following a business model originally developed by crack dealers.

Your daughter will also need makeup, as specified by strict written dance-studio guidelines, which require that, because these are young girls with flawless skin, they must wear a sufficient quantity of cosmetic products to cover a regulation volleyball court, or, to put it another way, Cher. Also your daughter's hair must be compacted into a bun, and it must be a very tight, dense, ballerina-style bun, held in place by weapons-grade hair gel to keep it from exploding due to the severe pressure exerted on it by your wife, who by this point, trust me, is not in a great mood.

Once your wife is convinced that your daughter is ready (allow nine hours) it's time to go to the recital, which will be in an auditorium containing hundreds and hundreds of people who are no more interested in watching your daughter dance than you are in watching their daughters dance. As you enter, you will be handed a program, and when you examine it, you will find that your daughter's first dance routine is near the beginning of the program, and her second routine is near the very end. In between will be roughly two thousand routines featuring other people's daughters.

You would think that, by sheer chance, there would come a time when your daughter's two dances would be close together, ideally near the beginning. But the dance studio makes sure this never happens, using the same computer scheduling program that the cable-TV company uses to make sure that the technician, for whom you have been waiting eleven hours, rings your doorbell only when you have just commenced pooping.

Clutching the program, you take your seat, which is near the back of the auditorium, because all the seats near the front have been claimed by Serious Dance Moms who got in line early, in some cases before their daughters were actually born. Finally the lights dim, the curtain goes up, and you begin to watch other people's daughters perform their routines. Each routine takes about three minutes, or, in Dance Recital Time, six years.

The most entertaining routines are the ones performed by three-year-old girls, usually dressed as something cute, such as bumblebees, so that everybody, even men who are not fathers of the dancers, goes "awwww." The bumblebees come out in a line, some looking excited to be out there, some terrified, some lost, some picking their cute little bumblebee noses. But when the music starts, an amazing thing happens: what had been a random-acting group of little girls suddenly transforms itself into a group of little girls who are continuing to act pretty much randomly. Some face the audience; some turn around, presenting the audience with their little bumblebee butts.

Meanwhile, offstage, their dance teacher is frantically gesturing, trying to remind them how their routine goes. If, for example, they're supposed to twirl, the teacher will twirl. One or two of the more alert bumblebees will notice, and they will twirl, usually in different directions. Other bumblebees, noticing this, will then twirl, so you have a chain reaction of twirling, along with a certain amount of falling down, standing still, and running offstage in tears. Then the music stops and everybody applauds heartily, and the bumblebees run off the stage, except for the ones who remain on the stage.

As I say, these are the more entertaining routines. Most of them, however, consist of other people's daughters prancing around more or less in unison to various styles of music that you would not listen to voluntarily, using the medium of dance to express universal human emotions such as love, fear, joy, despair, and prancing.

Then, finally, comes the moment you have been waiting for: You fall asleep. At some point after that you feel your wife's elbow, which is the signal that your daughter's first routine is about to begin. The lights come up, the music starts, and . . . There she is! You watch in amazement as she performs the routine she has practiced for so long. You are stunned. She's so beautiful! So poised! So confident! Your heart swells with pride. You can't believe that's really your daughter up there.

Then you realize that it's not, in fact, your daughter. At this distance they're hard to tell apart under all that makeup. You look around frantically, and just as the routine ends, you locate your daughter. Your heart re-swells with pride. Then you settle in for the long wait until her second routine. To pass the time, you think of ways in which the dance-recital experience could be improved. It goes without saying that beer vendors would be a huge help. But there is another element that I believe would make the dance-recital experience far more enjoyable for male audience members: competition.

Imagine this scene: Onstage is a group of daughters in tutus, prancing around to classical music, expressing the Hopefulness of Spring. Suddenly a second song, some kind of hideous inscrutable modern music, starts playing on top of the first one, and a new set of daughters appears onstage in leotards and starts slinking around to express Existential Angst. There are collisions. A member of the Hopefulness team goes down hard. A member of the Angst team takes a tutu to the eye. Then things get really exciting as a *third* song breaks out, this one hip-hop, and a third dance team charges onstage, dressed as tough streetwise urban gang members wearing enormous quantities of makeup. Now the stage is total chaos. The audience is also getting into it; parents are punching each other. Somebody knocks over a beer vendor. Wouldn't that be great? It would also help if there was a scoreboard, and some kind of ball.

Of course none of these things will happen. These are just daydreams you're having while you're waiting to see your daughter again, assuming you recognize her. By the time her second routine starts, she may have gone through puberty.

Finally, the recital ends, and you stagger outside. You reunite with your daughter and present her with the bouquet of flowers that your wife bought at the supermarket. You tell her she was wonderful, and you mean it sincerely. She was the best dancer you have ever seen. Assuming that was her.

Technology

There was a time when the human race did not have technology. This time was called "the 1950s." I was a child then, and it was horrible. There were only three TV channels, and at any given moment at least two of them were showing men playing the accordion in black and white. There was no remote control, so if you wanted to change the channel, you had to yell at your little brother, "Phil! Change the channel!" (In those days people named their children "Phil.")

Your household had one telephone, which weighed eleven pounds and could be used as a murder weapon. It was permanently tethered to the living-room wall, and you had to dial it by manually turning a little wheel, and if you got a long-distance call, you'd yell, "It's long distance!" in the same urgent tone you would use to yell "Fire!" Everybody would come sprinting into the living room, because in the 1950s long distance was more exciting than sex. In fact there *was* no sex in the 1950s, that I know of.

There were automobiles, but they lacked many of the features that automobiles have today, such as a working motor. In the Barry household, we had a series of cars named (these were all real Barry cars) the "Rambler," the "Minx," the "Metropolitan," and the "Valiant." You could rely on these cars—rain or shine, hot or cold—to not start. The "Metropolitan," in particular, was no more capable of internal combustion than of producing a litter of puppies.

There also were computers in those days, but they filled entire rooms and weighed many tons. An ill-advised effort by IBM to market one of these in the "laptop" configuration was abandoned when the first test user was converted into what the medical examiner's report described as "basically a human pizza twelve feet in diameter."

This pre-technology era was especially brutal for young people. We had no Wii. Mainly what we had to play with was rocks, which we had to throw at each other by hand. What few toys we had were lame, like the Slinky, which did basically one thing: go down stairs. And it did *that* only in the TV commercials, which apparently were filmed on a planet with much more gravity. Here on the Earth, the Slinky went down maybe two steps, then fell over on its side, twitched, and died, like a snake having a heart attack.

We also had the Wheel-O. This was a toy that, by federal law, was issued to every American boy and girl who was alive during the Eisenhower administration. The Wheel-O consisted of a red wheel and a wire frame:

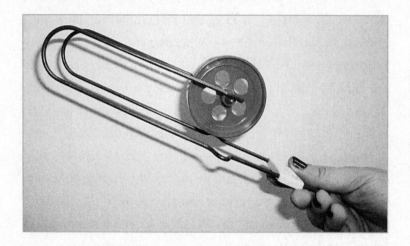

The wheel stuck to the frame because of magnetism, which was a new and much more exciting force back then. To play with your Wheel-O, you tilted the frame so the wheel rolled down, then up, then down, then up, and so on. Before you knew it, two minutes had flown by, and it was time to go outside and throw rocks.

The most technologically advanced toy I had was the Erector Set, which was a box containing hundreds of metal pieces, gears, bolts, nuts, washers, etc., along with instructions showing how to assemble these into projects such as a miniature Ferris wheel that actually rotated. This required many hours of effort, but I found that if I followed the instructions carefully, I learned something important: I could never, ever, make an object that looked anything like the miniature Ferris wheel in the instruction book. What I produced looked more like a tragic miniature building collapse. That is why I became an English major.

We have come a long way since the 1950s. Today we have technology up the wazoo,[1] and we use it constantly in our everyday lives. Consider, for example, my typical morning routine:

For openers, I sleep next to an alarm clock that is accurate to something like one jillionth of a second. This is because it receives wireless signals from the official U.S. atomic clock, which as its name suggests is a clock made out of atoms, making it very small and difficult to wind. Half the time the government scientists can't even find it. ("Dang! I think I sucked the atomic clock up my nose again!") But it's very accurate, so when I go to bed at night and set my alarm clock for 7 A.M., I know for a fact that in the morning I will be awakened at precisely 5:43 A.M., because that is when my dog, Lucy, decides that it's time to go out.

---

1. I mean this literally. Medical researchers at UCLA recently fitted a fifty-seven-year-old man with a working artificial wazoo.

Lucy is also part of the high-tech revolution: She contains a tiny implanted microchip, which can identify her if she runs off, which is not an unlikely scenario given that she has the IQ of a radish. Actually, that's not fair. If you feed and care for a radish, it will have the sense to stay with you. Whereas Lucy would leave in a heartbeat with anybody. A machete-wielding lunatic could come to our house, hack us to tiny pieces, then whistle to Lucy, and she would cheerfully follow him away, especially if he was holding her squeaky toy.

So anyway, at 5:43 A.M. sharp, according to the U.S. atomic clock, Lucy and I head out to the backyard so she can initiate the complex process of finding an acceptable place to poop. I think that while they're implanting chips in dogs, they should implant one in the dog's brain, assuming they can find it, that would allow you to make your dog poop by remote control. As it is, I have to wait while Lucy sniffs, one by one, every single odor molecule in our yard before settling on the exact spot where she has pooped 1,378 consecutive times.

In the old low-tech days, I would spend this idle backyard time standing around scratching myself with both hands. But now, thanks to technology, I scratch with just the one hand, while using the other one to be productive on my cell phone. With this amazing device, I can send and receive e-mail and text messages, surf the Internet, pay my bills, book flights, play games, take pictures, listen to music, watch TV shows—in short almost anything except reliably make or receive telephone calls. For some reason, cellular telephones lack that capability. It's as if they made a washing machine that mowed your lawn and made daiquiris, but if you put your actual clothes into it, they burst into flames.

But my point is that while Lucy is inhaling her way around the yard, I am using cell-phone technology to *get things done*. I am reading e-mails offering to sell me male-enhancement products so powerful that I will need a wheelbarrow to cart my privates around. I am also reading e-mails from available women on other continents who are hoping to strike up a friendship with me that could blossom into a deeper relationship with the promise—someday—of exchanging intimate personal financial data.

I can also use my phone to go to Facebook and Twitter to read messages and "tweets" from a vast network of people I do not really know, updating me on their random neural firings on such issues as what they are eating. In the old pre-technology days, it would have been almost impossible to replicate Facebook or Twitter. The closest you could get would be to mail dozens of postcards a day to everybody you knew, each with a brief message about yourself like: "Finally got that haircut I've been putting off." Or: "Just had a caramel frappuccino. Yum!"

The people receiving these postcards would have naturally assumed that you were a moron with a narcissism disorder. But today, thanks to Facebook and Twitter, you are seen as a person engaging in "social networking." As the technology improves, we'll reach the point when you don't even need a phone to socially network. You'll have some kind of device implanted in your brain so you can receive other people's brain waves directly as they occur. You will know *everything* about them. You will know when they *fart*.

Speaking of which: When Lucy finally decides, after much deliberation and a minimum of eight full clockwise rotations of her body, to poop on exactly the same spot for the 1,379th consecutive time, we head into the house. The sun isn't even up yet, and I have already, using handheld technology with just one hand, wasted more time than my father did in an entire day.

And I am just getting started. In the kitchen, I turn on a TV set that has hundreds of channels devoted to every conceivable subject including celebrity bunion removal.[2] I tune in to one of the literally dozens of news shows, all of which feature a format of 55 percent celebrities promoting things, 30 percent e-mails from viewers, and 15 percent YouTube videos showing bears jumping on trampolines. While I'm catching up on these developments, I turn on the programmable coffeemaker, which I hope that someday, perhaps by attending community college, I will learn to program. Then I take a breakfast "sausage" made of processed tofu from the freezer and pop it into the microwave oven, which in seconds converts it from a frozen, unappetizing gray cylinder into a piping hot unappetizing gray cylinder. It performs

---

2. This week: David Hasselhoff.

this culinary miracle by bombarding the frozen tofu with atomic radiation—the very same deadly force that, back in the 1950s, caused insects to mutate into savage monster killers the size of Charles Barkley, now harnessed by modern technology for peaceful breakfast purposes.

OK, that might not be 100 percent technically accurate. The truth is, I don't really know how my microwave oven works. I also don't know how my cell phone works, or my TV, or my computer, or my iPod, or my GPS, or my camera that puts nineteen thousand pictures inside a tiny piece of plastic, which is obviously NOT PHYSICALLY POSSIBLE, but there it is. Basically all I know about these devices is how to turn them on, and if they stop working, I know I should turn them off and then turn them back on, because usually this makes them resume working. If it doesn't, I know I need to buy a new device, because nobody in the entire world knows how to fix a broken one.

Don't get me wrong: I love technology. I don't want to go back to the days when people had to churn their own butter and make their own sausage by going out to the barn and personally slaughtering tofus. But it bothers me that I depend on so many things that operate on principles I do not remotely understand, and which might not even be real.

Take "digital" technology. At some point (I think during the Clinton administration) all media—photographs, TV, movies, music, oven thermometers, pornography, doorbells, etc.—became "digital." If you ask a technical expert what this means, he or she will answer that the information is, quote, "broken down into ones and zeros." Which sounds good, doesn't it? Ones and zeros! Those are digits, all right!

But here's the problem. Say you're watching a TV show. Say it's *24*, starring Kiefer Sutherland as Jack Bauer, the angst-ridden lone-wolf federal agent who protects America from terrorism by sooner or later causing the violent death of pretty much everybody he meets. If you study this show carefully, you will notice something curious: *Jack Bauer never goes to the bathroom.* That's why he's so ridden with angst.

But the other curious thing you will notice is that no matter how close you get to the TV screen—even if you get one inch away and examine the picture (I have done this) with a magnifying glass, so that any given one of Jack Bauer's nostrils is the size of the Lincoln Tunnel—*you cannot see any ones or zeros.* They're lying to us about that.

Why is this? My theory—and bear in mind that I have won several journalism awards—is that the "experts" don't really know how any of this technology works either. All they know is that it arrives here in boxes from China. I don't know where the Chinese are getting it, but I do know that they're not making it themselves. I have been to China, and if the Chinese had any grasp of technology, they would have better toilets.

So the bottom line is that we have become totally dependent in our daily lives on technology that nobody understands and that could be coming from (this is speculation) space. What if all this technology is some kind of sneak alien invasion force? What if one day all these devices rose up and attacked us? What if, for example, all the Bluetooth phone earpieces in the world suddenly sprouted drill bits and bored into people's brains?

OK, that particular example would actually be fine. But you see my point, don't you? If so, could you send me an e-mail or tweet explaining it?

No, seriously, my point is that technology is a blessing, but it is also a serious potential threat to humanity in general. Somebody needs to look into this. I'd do it myself, but right now I can't. My atomic-clock alarm is going off, signaling that it's 7 A.M., which means it's time for me to go back to bed.

Solving the
Celebrity Problem

don't want to toot my own horn, but I am something of a minor celebrity.

"How minor?" you ask.

I'll give you an example. Often, when I'm in a public place such as an airport gate area, I'll notice that one of the other passengers keeps looking at me. Finally this person will come over, and we'll have a conversation like the following (I have had this conversation literally dozens of times):

PERSON: I hate to bother you, but I'm a *huge* fan of your writing.
ME: Thanks! No bother at all!
PERSON: And my kids LOVED *Hoot*.

ME: Um, you're thinking of Carl Hiaasen. We both write for the *Miami Herald*. I'm Dave Barry.

PERSON (HUGELY EMBARRASSED): Oh my God, I am *so sorry*.

ME: It's OK, really. Carl's a good friend.

PERSON: I'm a big fan of your writing, too!

ME: Thanks.

PERSON: Obviously I am lying.

(The person never actually says that last part out loud; there is no need.)

I'm not saying that I'm as big a celebrity as Brad Pitt, although when you look at the following side-by-side comparison of Brad and me in chart form, you'll see that there's not really such a huge difference:[1]

Celebrity Indicator	Brad Pitt	Me
Gets recognized in public	Yes	Sort of
Is wanted carnally by every woman on Earth	Yes	No
Has a sewage lifting station named for him in Grand Forks, N.D.[1]	No	Yes

---

1. Motto: "Gateway to Whatever Is on the Other Side of Grand Forks, N.D."

Over the years, my celebrity status has provided me with certain "perks" that are not available to the public. For example, I was once a Grand Marshal in the Main Street Parade at Walt Disney World. This is a great honor, and if you ever get offered a chance to do it, you should definitely refuse. Number one, you have to wear mouse ears, so if you're over six years old, you look like an idiot. Number two, despite the fact that you are the Grand Marshal of the parade, *you aren't really in the parade*. At least I wasn't.

What happened was, they put me and my co-marshal, author Ridley Pearson, into an antique fire truck along with Daisy Duck and Clarabelle the Cow. I have nothing against either of these veteran Disney characters, but let's be honest, their careers are not currently sizzling, especially in the case of Clarabelle, who hasn't had a hit cartoon since roughly the Civil War. (Also, not to be catty, but she has had a *lot* of work done on her udder.)

So anyway, Ridley and I and our families got into this fire truck with Daisy and Clarabelle, and then they sent us out into the Magic Kingdom, where literally fifty thousand people had been waiting restlessly in the heat to see the legendary Main Street Parade with all its spectacular floats. The problem was that *the parade did not follow us*. I don't know if it was a prank or what, but for some reason the parade floats remained back in the staging area for at least ten more minutes. This meant that we were out there basically naked, with no float cover, two idiots in rodent ears sitting next to a B-list duck and cow in a fire truck creeping through this vast sea of restless expectant tourists at the speed of a tectonic plate. It was horrible. We had been instructed to wave, so we grimly waved for the whole parade route (roughly eighty-two miles) but hardly anybody waved back. You could see the puzzlement on their faces as they put down their video cameras and asked each other: "Who are these dorks?" And: "Where's the actual parade?" And: "Is that Carl Hiaasen next to Clarabelle?"

Another "perk" that comes with being a minor celebrity is that I occasionally have the opportunity to interact with celebrities who are actually famous. For example, I once shared a microphone with Bruce Springsteen. This happened because I belong to a rock band called The Rock Bottom Remainders, which consists mostly of authors. Our biggest celebrity author is Stephen King, although he keeps a fairly low profile. For example, once I went to a baseball game with him, and he wore a ball cap, so most people didn't recognize him. Just before the game started, the actor David Birney arrived and sat two rows in front of us. The woman sitting behind him wanted to get his autograph, but she didn't have a pen. So she turned around, all excited, and asked if anybody had a pen. She borrowed one, used it to get David Birney's autograph, then handed the pen back to: Stephen King.

Anyway, The Rock Bottom Remainders get together once a year to play benefit concerts on behalf of literacy. You may have noticed that for some time now, literacy has been in a steep decline. I'm not saying the Remainders are totally responsible for this, but we're probably a factor, because as a band, we suck. We routinely play entire songs without ever reaching full agreement on the question of what specific key we are in. So when people hear us perform, their reaction often is: "Maybe literacy isn't such a great idea."

Anyway, one time the Remainders were performing at an event in Los Angeles, and Bruce Springsteen was there, and he joined us onstage for one song. As it happened, he and I shared a microphone, just a couple of celebrities chilling together. Here is a verbatim transcript of everything that was said between us:

ME: G-L-O-R-I-A!
BRUCE SPRINGSTEEN: Gloria!
ME: G-L-O-R-I-A!
BRUCE SPRINGSTEEN: Gloria!
ME: I'm gonna shout it all night!
BRUCE SPRINGSTEEN: Gloria!
ME: Gonna sing it *every*place!
BRUCE SPRINGSTEEN: Gloria!

So to be totally honest, Bruce didn't say anything to me except "Gloria!" But in the time we spent together, I could tell that, despite his celebrity, he's a regular guy, a guy who puts his pants on just like everybody else, with the zipper in the front.

Another perk that comes with being a celebrity is that you get to go into VIP areas. These are areas at clubs or events where only celebrities are allowed to go, so they'll have some privacy while they engage in exclusive celebrity activities such as standing around. In my experience, this is mainly what VIPs do in their areas: They stand around. It's not a significantly different experience from standing around in a civilian area. But for some reason, whenever there's any kind of exclusive area, people develop a *fierce* desire to stand around inside it.

It reminds me of lobsters. If you've ever looked at a tank of lobsters in a restaurant, you've noticed that most of them tend to clump together in one corner of the tank, even though they'd have more room if they spread out. They have decided, for whatever lobster reason, that this corner is more desirable than the other corners, where you might find one or two lobsters who weren't allowed into the VIP corner because they are *losers*.

I witnessed a dramatic demonstration of the pulling power of the VIP area during a party at the 2000 Republican convention in Philadelphia. Political conventions are excellent places to observe VIP-area-lust, because they're teeming with high-level Washington-dwelling people who have chosen careers in public service specifically to avoid having any contact with the actual public. These people *live* for VIP treatment. Do you think that the Secretary of Commerce is motivated by an interest in the activities of the Department of Commerce? Don't be a moron. Nobody even knows what the Department of Commerce *does*, including the employees, who spend their days planning elaborate pranks on the Department of Agriculture. No, the reason you want to be Secretary of Commerce is you get to ride around Washington in a limousine containing zero members of the public.

At a national political convention, you have hundreds of people who consider themselves at least as important as the Secretary of Commerce. If it's a Democratic convention, you also have dozens of A-list Hollywood and music celebrities. (If it's a Republican convention, you have Bo Derek.) Also you have swarms of lower-ranking Washington minions with titles like Deputy Assistant to the Associate Deputy Assistant Chief of Staff who are trying to move up the ladder to Deputy Associate to the Assistant Acting Deputy Assistant Undersecretary.

So at the conventions you have thousands of these highly status-conscious people swarming around, and every night all of them try to get into the same two or three exclusive parties. These parties are a HUGE deal, and it is truly pathetic the way people will whine and beg and grovel to get in. I know, because I'm one of these people. I have attended every political convention from 1984 on, and I estimate that I spend 93 percent of my time, as a professional journalist, trying to get into exclusive parties. Usually I fail, but every now and then I succeed, and it's amazing, the elation you feel when you talk your way past the gatekeepers, leaving behind the pathetic losers standing around outside, because you know that once you get inside the exclusive party you're going to have wild monkey sex with dozens of A-list

Hollywood celebrities. (Or, if it's a Republican convention, Bo Derek.)

No, seriously, all you do at these parties is stand around. Often you don't even see any A-list celebrities, because they're standing around in an even *more* exclusive area inside the party, set aside for VIPs more important than you. Which means that, on some level, *you're still a loser.*

This was the situation I encountered at the 2000 Republican convention in Philadelphia. I was with a posse of five newspaper cartoonists, and we had managed, with great effort, to grovel our way into an exclusive party in a nightclub, only to discover that we were in the *outer* VIP area. There was an *inner* VIP area (possibly containing Bo Derek) that we couldn't get into.

We were wandering around when we came across a room with a platform in the middle, about the size of a Ping-Pong table, raised two feet off the floor. For some reason, possibly related to beer consumption, we decided to turn this into our own VIP area. We climbed onto the platform and stood there, six guys on a platform. Whenever anybody walked past, we'd shout, "Sorry! VIP area! You can't come up here!"

As you can imagine, this caused people to leave the room immediately. So for a while it was just the six of us in our VIP area. But then an amazing thing happened: Dick "Dick" Armey, who at that time was the majority leader of the U.S. House of Representatives, entered the room. We invited him to join us. Incredibly, he agreed.

So now we had an actual VIP on our VIP platform. This had an immediate and powerful effect on the people entering the room: They'd see the House majority leader, and *they wanted to be on the platform*. Of course we didn't let just anyone join us. We were total assholes about it. We admitted only those who belonged to one of three elite groups: (1) people whom Dick Armey knew personally; (2) people whom we knew personally; and (3) women.

Even so, within minutes we had easily thirty people jammed together on this smallish platform in the middle of an otherwise basically empty room, with more people pleading to be allowed on. Granted, some of these people just wanted to be on the platform as a goof. But I think the majority wanted to be up there because they genuinely believed it was more desirable to be squashed into a VIP area than to stand comfortably in a non-VIP area three feet away.

Why do people act this way? For the same reason lobsters do: They have brains the size of sesame seeds.

Which brings us to reality television. As a minor celebrity, I am concerned about the effect it is having on the overall celebrity population. Consider the following celebrity news item, which I found on the *People* magazine Internet site:

KARDASHIAN SISTERS NOT
BARING ALL . . . YET

For now, it's keeping it on with the Kardashians.
The three TV reality star sisters—Kim, 28;

So essentially in this item *People* is reporting that Kim Kardashian has posted an item on her blog denying an untrue rumor that most people would never have heard of if Kim Kardashian hadn't posted it on her blog in the first place. In other words, nothing happened. This is considered news because Kim Kardashian is what is known as a "reality-show personality." She has appeared on *Dancing with the Stars* as well as in a widely distributed homemade sex video. It goes without saying that she also has a fragrance line. Kim and her sisters Khloe and Kourtney are the stars of the reality show *Keeping Up with the Kardashians*, which is about all the fascinating celebrity things that you do when you are a Kardashian, such as eat. Also appearing on the show are other members of the Kardashian Klan, including their mom and their stepfather, Olympic decathlon champion Bruce Jenner, whose son, Brody Jenner, is also a reality-show personality, having appeared on a number of reality shows and dated several other reality-show personalities, including Nicole Richie, who was on a reality show with Paris Hilton.[2]

My point is that thanks to reality TV, all of these people are now

2. Paris and Nicole both have fragrance lines.

celebrities, despite the fact that *the only one who has ever actually done anything* is Bruce Jenner.[3] And the Kardashians are just a tiny part of the vast, ever-expanding reality-show industry, which is constantly vomiting out new celebrities, adding to the strain on our nation's already overburdened VIP-area resources.

Also contributing to the celebrity glut is the disturbing phenomenon of "celebrity DJs." These are the people who put on headphones and play records while adjusting knobs with expressions of great intensity, as if they are performing a particularly challenging violin solo, when in fact they are PLAYING A FREAKING RECORD, which requires NO MORE ARTISTIC TALENT THAN REHEATING A BURRITO IN A MICROWAVE OVEN.

I apologize for using capital letters, but this is a serious problem. America has become a nation where more citizens can name the contestants on *American Idol* than can name their own important government leaders, such as the Secretary of Commerce.

We need to do something about the celebrity surplus, and I have an idea, which I got from agriculture. Think about it: What do we do when our farms produce surplus wheat, and it starts to pile up in grain silos? We export it to other countries! Do you see where I'm going with this? That's right: We need to *start putting minor celebrities into grain silos*.

---

3. I don't want to toot my own horn, but in 1997, when I was in Los Angeles on a book tour, I was on a show called *Home & Family* during which I spent several minutes sitting on a couch with Bruce Jenner, as well as an Italian cookbook author and a complete set of quintuplets. I don't know if any of them has a fragrance line, but I would not rule it out.

If that turns out to be legally questionable, we should export them. This would not be difficult. All we'd have to do is park a cruise ship in Los Angeles and announce a new reality show called *Celebrity Cruise with the Stars*. Within minutes there would be Kardashians storming up the gangway. As soon as the ship was full, we'd untie it and send it steaming off to someplace that doesn't produce enough celebrities of its own, such as Asia. Granted, at some point these people might try to get back to the United States. But that is exactly why we have a navy.

By following this program, America could get back to a saner and simpler time; a time when being a celebrity *meant* something; a time when it was easier for veteran traditional minor celebrities such as Clarabelle and myself to get into popular restaurants. I know I speak for both of us when I assure you that we will not take this privilege lightly. As celebrities, we will conduct ourselves with dignity and never knowingly pose naked for *Playboy* without adequate compensation. We recognize that we are role models for the public. This is why I always make sure that I wash my hands after I pee in a public restroom. I don't want somebody recognizing me and going around telling people, "Hey, you know who doesn't wash his hands after he pees? Carl Hiaasen!" Because as I say, Carl is a friend.

Tips for Visiting Miami

~~~~~~~~~~~~~~~~~~~

No. 1: Are You Insane?

Some years ago I proposed a new tourism-promotion slogan for Miami. I even had a bumper sticker made. It said:

> ## COME BACK TO MIAMI!
> We Weren't Shooting at *You*.

For some reason this slogan never caught on with Miami's tourism industry. Which is a shame, because we need to improve our image. According to a poll by the Zogby organization, 67 percent of Americans agree either "somewhat" or "strongly" with the statement that "Miami is plagued by crime." This is very upsetting to those of us who live here and love our city. It makes us want to visit every single one of those 67 percent of Americans personally, so we can tell them what Miami is *really* like, and then kill them with machetes.

But seriously, we are sick and tired of being saddled with the hackneyed, outdated *Miami Vice* and *Scarface* image of Miami—a city crawling with homicidal maniac drug dealers like Al Pacino, casually committing horrendous acts of violence and, worse, speaking with ludicrously fake Cuban accents. The truth is that only a small percentage of Miami's population consists of violent criminals, and the bulk of those are elected officials. The rest of us Miamians are regular people, just like the people in your town: We work hard, try to raise our kids right, and are always ready to help out our neighbors by laying down covering fire when they go outside to get their newspapers.

I'll grant you that in the past Miami has had some problems with "putting out the welcome mat" for tourists. I'd say the low point came in 1994, when a group of Norwegians, headed for a vacation in the Bahamas, made a common rookie-visitor mistake: They landed at Miami International Third World Airport (Motto: "You Can Have Your Luggage When You Pry It From Our Cold, Dead Fingers"). Most travel experts recommend that even if your final destination is Miami, it's better to fly to an airport in some other city—if necessary, Seattle—and take a cab from there. Or, as *Savvy Air Traveler* magazine suggests, "simply jump out of the plane while it's still over the Atlantic."

Nonetheless these Norwegian tourists landed at MIA, where

they boarded a free courtesy shuttle van that was supposed to take them to a hotel. So far, so good. Unfortunately, the van was then boarded by two men who diverted it and robbed the Norwegians at gunpoint. That is correct: *Their hotel courtesy van was hijacked.* This story got BIG play in Norway, which does not have a lot of violent crime. If there were a TV crime show called *CSI: Norway*, most of the cases would involve improperly labeled herring.

So the van hijacking was definitely a "black eye" for Miami tourism. It did not help that in the same year, there was another unfortunate, highly publicized incident involving a European tourist. This was a German who spent the night at a hotel near the Miami airport. When he checked out the next morning, he complained about a bad smell in his room. So a maid went to check it out. She looked under the bed, and, to her horror, she found: an Amway representative.

No, seriously, what the maid found under the bed was even worse: a human corpse. This was not a recently deceased corpse; the police concluded it had been there for quite a while.

As you might imagine, this was another story that became a big media deal back in the tourist's home country. The Germans are known for being finicky about cleanliness. They might let it slide if a hotel housekeeping staff failed to notice a dust bunny or two under the bed, but they draw the line at decayed corpses. If you find a corpse under the bed at a German hotel, you can be sure it's a *fresh* corpse. Once again, Miami looked bad.

But my point is, these stories *took place during a different era*, specifically: the past. Miami today is a completely different city. What would you say if I told you that, since the year 2000, the city's overall rate of violent crime is down 17.3 percent, and crime against tourists is down by 36.8 percent? If you would say, "You are totally making those numbers up," you would be correct. But I'm pretty sure things are better.

I'm not saying Miami is Disney World. As in any other large urban area, you have to use your common sense to avoid potentially dangerous situations. To give you an idea what I mean by "potentially dangerous situations," here's the beginning of a *Miami Herald* story from November 2006: "A manhunt is on for fifteen men who crashed a baby shower in a rented hall, killed a partygoer, and wounded four other guests with AK-47 assault rifles."

That is correct: There was a shootout, featuring assault rifles, *at a baby shower*. It is not uncommon for tempers to flare at ceremonial gatherings in Miami; there was once a shootout in a funeral home here *during a wake*. Other events that can be "iffy" from a safety standpoint in Miami include birthday parties, football games, proms, nightclubs, Halloween, July Fourth, Christmas, and of course New Year's Eve, which in Miami involves more gunfire than the Battle of the Bulge, although to be fair most of it is *happy* gunfire.

But as long as you avoid these dangerous situations, you'll be perfectly safe in Miami, provided that you watch out for traffic. This is not as easy as it sounds. In Miami, traffic can appear anywhere—on the streets, of course, but also on sidewalks, as well as in parks, front yards, restaurants, hotel lobbies, and swimming pools. You may think I'm exaggerating, but that's only because you don't watch the local TV news in Miami, which routinely features images of cars that have been driven into what we usually think of as non-automotive environments such as buildings. At risk of reinforcing an unfortunate stereotype, I have to point out that many of these cars, at the time of impact, were being piloted by senior citizens possessing the same level of awareness of their surroundings as a salami sandwich.

To cite just one example: In 2008, police in Miami stopped a seventy-three-year-old man who was driving a Chevrolet Cobalt. This in itself is not unusual; police often, for one reason or another, stop older drivers. What was unusual was where they stopped this man:

Runway 9 of Miami International Airport.

Really. The man had somehow, without noticing it, burst through an airport-perimeter gate, and when the police caught up with him, he was driving on the runway, apparently unaware that he was doing anything wrong. ("Is there a problem, Officer?") This incident really makes me wonder about the priorities of our airport-security people. I mean, when *I* go to an airport, they won't let me near an airplane with *shampoo*. And this guy was out there with a *Cobalt*.[1]

---

1. Maybe he had it in one of those clear plastic bags.

My point is, when you're in Miami, you should be very alert if you're in a place where a car might hit you, which is pretty much anywhere below the fourth floor. And you definitely shouldn't attempt to drive yourself in Miami, because odds are you'd make some foolish tourist mistake such as stop for a red light, which means you'd be rear-ended by a vehicle going upwards of eighty miles per hour driven by a motorist with no insurance but a minimum of two firearms.

That leaves public transportation. Here there is good news and bad news. The good news is, Miami does have public transportation. The bad news is, if you ride on it, there is a chance that you will encounter dangerous marine life. I say this because of an incident that occurred in 2009 on Miami's Metromover, which is a free automated "people mover" that makes a loop around downtown Miami. One evening at rush hour, two men boarded the Metromover *with a live, six-foot-long nurse shark.* The men had apparently caught the shark in Biscayne Bay and were using public transportation to take it downtown to sell it.

One of the people who saw the shark, according to the story in the *Miami Herald*, was a twenty-four-year-old musician named Mae Singerman, who was getting ready to do a show on the Metromover platform. The *Herald* quoted Singerman as saying: "The door opened and the shark was sitting by the front of the door. I didn't see a reason to call police. It's Miami. Stranger things have happened."

True. Still, not everybody was blasé about the shark. One of

the commuters who boarded the Metromover, Sandy Goodrich, sent me an e-mail stating that, as a native Miamian, she thought she had seen everything, until she saw the shark.

"Unbelievable," she wrote. "Only in Miami!" Attached to her e-mail was a photo she'd taken with her cell phone, "so that my son would believe that there was actually a shark on the train."

She said the shark was definitely alive, although it was not doing well. Sharks are hardy creatures, but they do not thrive on public transportation. The men got off the Metromover a few stops later and took the shark to a fish wholesaler, offering to sell it for $10. The wholesaler declined, and the men left the shark—which at this point had kicked the bucket—on a downtown Miami street, where it lay for hours before the authorities removed it. It attracted some attention, but not as much as if it had been lying on a street in, say, Des Moines. The *Herald* quoted a local resident as saying: "It was a relief that it was a shark. When I first saw it, I thought it was a body because of all the shootings that have been going on. I was surprised and happy because of my concern for human life."

So this was actually a feel-good story, Miami-style: Against all odds, it wasn't a human body! Still, the fact remains that—this bears repeating—there was a live shark on the Metromover. And had it been a little *more* alive, there is a very real possibility that it could actually have bitten somebody. We could have had a shark attack on a commuter train! Wouldn't that have been *great?*

No, wait, I mean: Wouldn't that have been tragic? Yes it would, which is why I'm recommending that you exercise caution when boarding public transportation, and by "exercise caution" I mean "carry a speargun."

You should also watch out when you *leave* public transportation, because then you will be in one of the most dangerous areas in all of South Florida, namely: outdoors. We have a lot of extreme wildlife here. Over the years I have personally encountered, just in my neighborhood, several alligators, hundreds of poison toads, mutant, heavily armored five-inch grasshoppers that cannot be killed with a hammer, irate, hissing, needle-toothed lizards the size of Chihuahuas, and huge spiders that appear to be wearing the pelts of raccoons. I have also had numerous sphincter-disrupting encounters with snakes, including one that, when I noticed it, was coiled up approximately six inches away from me *on my office desk*, which is how my office chair came to have a stain.

We also have a growing population of unwelcome out-of-town wildlife species that have come here and clearly intend to stay. Two invasive species in particular have caused serious concern: Burmese pythons, and New Yorkers.

The New Yorkers have been coming for years, which is weird because pretty much all they do once they get to Florida is bitch about how everything here sucks compared to the earthly paradise that is New York. They continue to root, loudly, for the Jets, the Knicks, the Mets, and the Yankees; they never stop declaring, loudly, that in New York the restaurants are better, the stores are nicer, the people are smarter, the public transportation is free of sharks, etc.

The Burmese pythons are less obnoxious, but just as alarming in their own way. These are snakes that started out as pets of Miami residents, until one day these residents stopped smoking crack and said, "Jesus H. Christ! We're living with a giant snake!" So they let the pythons go, and a lot of them ended up out in the Everglades, which is basically Las Vegas for pythons. They've been engaging in wild python reproductive sex out there for years; wildlife biologists estimate that there are now more than one hundred thousand of them. They can grow to be longer than twenty feet, and they don't have any natural enemies, so they're eating all the other Everglades animals. The wildlife authorities are desperately trying to figure out what to do about this. My preference would be to use tactical nuclear weapons, but this would never fly with the wildlife community, which regards the Everglades as a precious ecosystem, even though to the naked civilian eye it is a giant festering stinkhole of rotting muck.

The more ecological alternative would be to introduce some kind of predator that would counteract the pythons. The question is, what kind of creature would be able to hold its own against these monstrous snakes? The obvious answer, which I'm sure has already occurred to you, is: New Yorkers. You'd take a batch of them out to the dead center of the Everglades and release them, and they'd immediately start complaining, loudly, about how there was no decent pizza out there, and how if New York had a vast trackless swamp, it would be WAY better than the Everglades, and so on. Pretty soon the pythons would get tired of this, and leave. Or, eat the New Yorkers. Either way is fine with me.

So to summarize your tips for visiting Miami:

- Don't fly here.
- Don't drive.
- Don't take public transportation.
- Don't walk.
- Don't go outside.

- Avoid human contact in general, *especially* baby showers.
- Whatever you do, do NOT come during hurricane season, which runs from June through the following June.

Other than these basic safety precautions, my only advice is: Have fun! Because Miami really is a fun town, once you adjust to it. I moved here in 1986 from the United States, and I've come to love it. In fact, if you visit, you might find yourself in my "neck of the woods." You might even see me outside, picking up my newspaper!

If so, duck.

Dog Ownership for Beginners

Introduction

Becoming a first-time dog-owner is a big step. It's like getting married, except that your new spouse will want to have sex with you, whereas your new dog will want to have sex with you *and* your furniture.

But make no mistake: When you get a dog, you're entering into a serious long-term relationship. A dog is a companion that, if you feed it and pet it and pretend that you sincerely want to take away its ball, will give you, in return, totally unqualified love. You could be Charles Manson, or Hitler, or even a lawyer who advertises on television, and your dog will still think you're the greatest thing ever. This tells you something very important about dogs: *They are not very bright.*

This is actually good. The last thing you want is a smart dog. My friends Buzz and Libby Burger once had a smart dog, and it was a nightmare. She was an Afghan hound named Doodle, and she did not care to take orders or be in any way confined. This was a problem because not only was she more intelligent than anybody in reality television, but she was also capable of land speeds in excess of three hundred miles per hour. If Libby and Buzz wanted to go out for dinner at 7 P.M., they had to start at 3 P.M. attempting to lure Doodle into the house using elaborate charades involving treats, fake departures, disguises, professional actors, computers, helicopters, holograms, live chickens, etc. Doodle would watch these goings-on, clearly amused, until Buzz or Libby had crept within one step of being close enough to grab her, then *whoosh* she'd dematerialize, Wile-E.-Coyote style, leaving Buzz or Libby grasping a cloud of Doodle-shaped dust as Doodle herself disappeared into the woods to manage her global hedge fund or whatever the hell she did in there.

That's not the kind of dog you want. You want a dog that will run headfirst at full speed into a wall chasing a ball that you have only pretended to throw. You want a dog that will do this ten consecutive times, and still, on your eleventh fake throw, launch itself at the wall with undiminished enthusiasm. You want a dog that considers you brilliant because of all the amazing things you can do, such as open a door; a dog that worships you as a treat-dispensing god; a dog that, when you have an intestinal flu and reek like a Hong Kong Dumpster because you have not showered or changed pajamas or brushed your teeth in four days, and you are crouched in the bathroom spewing random fluids and semi-solids from every orifice you possess, your dog is right there next to you, wagging its tail and licking you and just generally doing everything it can to communicate the message: "Wow! You have *never smelled more interesting!*"

Smell is very important to dogs. They have extremely sensitive noses, and they use their sense of smell to gather and process important information about the world around them, as follows: "Hey! A smell!" "Hey! Another smell!" "Hey! ANOTHER smell!" etc. You'd think that, at some point, the dog would grasp the fact that there are a lot of smells in the world, and move on. But that's because you don't have a dog yet.

What Kind of Dog Should You Get?

This is a complex question, and you need to consider many factors before you arrive at the correct answer, which is: A big dog.

What do I mean by "a big dog"? I mean "a dog that can knock over a standard-sized elderly woman it has never seen before because it is so happy to meet her." You do not want one of those yappy gerbil-sized dogs that travel as carry-on luggage and are always nervous because at any moment they could be eaten by grasshoppers. These are unhappy, angry dogs, because they know in their tiny gerbil hearts that everybody except their immediate owners hates them.

The sole advantage of small dogs is that they are portable. My wife and I once attended a New Year's Eve party at a swank private club on South Beach, and as we entered we saw a woman in a pretty much nonexistent dress carrying a small dog *in the cleavage of her breasts*, which I suspect were artificial inasmuch as any given one of them was the size of a Toyota Camry. The dog was a Yorkshire terrier, although this particular woman had enough capacity for a mature Rottweiler. You would think that a cleavage-dwelling dog would be happy, but this one was just as neurotic as any other small dog. I know, because I observed it closely until my wife made me stop.

But unless you have reason to transport your dog in your bazoomage, you want a large dog. You should get it at a rescue shelter, where it has been sitting around building up a huge throbbing storehouse of love, which it will lavish on you in a lifelong outpouring of affection, loyalty, and—above all—drool.

Preparing Your Home for Your New Dog

Dogs are descended from wolf-like animals that roamed in packs millions of years ago, when most of North America was covered by thick virgin forest, which is gone now because the dogs chewed it into spit-covered splinters. Modern dogs have retained this powerful chewing instinct, and will spend countless hours chewing on random objects. It's basically their hobby, kind of like Sudoku, only not as pointless.

So before you introduce your new dog to your home, you need to remove all chewable objects, including shoes, clothing, rugs, draperies, chairs, sofas, slow-moving children, and anything that has a plug. In fact it might be a good idea, before introducing the dog to your home, to introduce it, late at night, to somebody else's home; you can visit it there until it gets over the chewing phase, which typically lasts until about fifteen minutes before the dog's death.

If you're feeling crazy and decide to bring the dog into your own personal home, you need to learn:

How to Train Your Dog

You should start with house-training, which is important because dogs will try to "mark" your house as their territory by urinating on it, much as members of Congress put their names on buildings that taxpayers have paid for.

The key to successful house-training is to *lead by example*. Wait until your dog is watching you, then declare, in a calm yet authoritative voice: "Time to drain the lizard!" Immediately stride outside, urinate on your lawn, and reward yourself with a treat. Repeat these steps until the dog grasps the concept or you run out of beer.

Other useful commands to teach your dog are "stay," "heel," "remove your snout from that person's groin," "stop humping the Barcalounger," "do not bark violently for two straight hours at inanimate objects such as a flowerpot," "do not eat poop," and "if you must eat poop, then at least refrain from licking my face afterward."

To teach these commands to your dog, you need three things: (1) patience; (2) consistency; and (3) a dog from another planet. Earth-based dogs, at least in my experience, lack the requisite number of brain cells to learn them. The only trick I've ever been able to teach any of my dogs is "shake hands," which is not particularly useful. If Lassie were one of my dogs, when little Timmy got trapped in the quicksand and shouted, "Go get help, girl!" Lassie would sit at the edge of the quicksand pit and give Timmy high fives on the top of his head with her paw until he disappeared beneath the muck. Then, her work done, she'd trot briskly away, on the alert for her next mission. ("Hey! A smell!")

Feeding Your Dog

What kind of dog food is best for your dog? Many dog owners have strong views on this subject, which is one way you can tell they are insane. The best food for your dog is: brown dog food.

Oh, sure, you'll see TV ads claiming that a certain brand is superior, as evidenced by the fact that the dog in the commercial is enthusiastically chowing down on it. But what these ads fail to tell you is that the same dog would chow down, with equal enthusiasm, on any other brand of dog food, or any brand of cat food, or an actual cat, or a pair of soiled underpants, or the Declaration of Independence, or a clarinet.

Dogs did not get where they are today by being picky eaters. Back in prehistoric times, they were competing with the rest of their pack for food, and if they came across, say, the decaying carcass of a mastodon, they had to snatch whatever piece they could, because if they didn't, some other dog would. They'd swallow the piece quickly, and then, if it didn't agree with them, they'd simply throw it back up later, and some other dog would eat it. Or maybe the same dog would eat it again, because, as we have established, dogs are not the nuclear physicists of the animal kingdom. In this manner a pack of dogs could transport a single rancid mastodon rectum thousands of miles.

In modern times dogs still operate on the principle that you should eat first and worry later about whether what you ate was edible. My current dog, Lucy, eats, among many other things, photo albums. The first time she did this, we told her she was Bad, which made her feel very sorry and press herself into the floor like a big hairy remorseful worm. But a few days later she ate *another* photo album. Again she felt terribly guilty, but she obviously believed, in what passes for her mind, that she had no choice, because if *she* didn't eat the album, another dog might, and that was a chance she simply could not afford to take.

Brushing Your Dog's Teeth

Don't be an idiot.

Playing with Your Dog

It's important to play with your dog, because otherwise it will become bored and develop an OxyContin habit. Here are some good games for you and your dog:

Fetch: Show the dog a ball, then throw it. The dog will run after it and pick it up. Now try to get the dog to bring it back. Ha-ha! Be prepared for hours of rollicking fun.

Keep Away: Your dog will have at least one object that it considers to be highly desirable, such as a filthy saliva-drenched chew toy or the femur of a UPS driver. Wait until the dog is chewing on this object, then sneak up and, with a swift but authoritative motion, snatch the object away, hold it up in front of the dog, and say, "This is *mine*, do you understand? MINE!!" Your dog will become agitated and try to get the object back, but you must never give it back, ever. You must take it to your *grave*, or the dog will win.

Chess: This is another game where you should be able to establish your dominance. Do not let the dog go first.

Emptying Your Dog's Impacted Anal Scent Glands

See "Brushing Your Dog's Teeth."

Conclusion

As we have seen, dog ownership is really just a matter of common sense. If you follow the procedures described in this article, your dog will reward you with a lifetime of love and loyalty in the form of lying on the floor right next to you silently emitting nuclear farts.

Another way to go is tropical fish.

My Hollywood Career

The Big Dumpster

n the field of professional writing, the best job is screenwriter. Why? As the late William Shakespeare—who wrote *Romeo and Juliet* and *Romeo and Juliet 2: The Rising*—put it: "Dollars per word, baby."

Think about it. If you write a novel, it has to contain tens of thousands of words, because you have to keep describing things to give the reader a mental picture of what's going on:

CHAPTER ONE

Steve Weemer stood before the door, pondering his next move. He was a tall man, standing a rangy six-feet-three, with broad shoulders and longish sandy hair flecked with gray framing a craggy face and eyes the same piercing blue color as a chunk of ice that falls to Earth after breaking loose from the leaking commode of a commercial airliner at thirty-five thousand feet. The door was Belgian oak veneer and stood six-feet-eight, the U.S. standard height for residences.

Weemer sighed and placed his gnarled hand on the doorknob, which was the color of silver, although it was actually steel with a chrome finish. Turning the knob clockwise to retract the latch, he gently pushed the door open and stepped into the room. It was rectangular, furnished with Ikea furniture that had been assembled from thousands of pieces of compressed particle board that Ikea had somehow packed into cartons no thicker than a pizza box, although Weemer knew each of those cartons contained upwards of 2,500 individual pieces and weighed as much as a Buick LaCrosse. Weemer had assembled much of this furniture himself. That's how his hands had become gnarled.

Corinne was waiting for him.

She was in her early forties, an attractive woman with a trim figure, gray-green eyes, and hair that was the warm brown color of No. 58 Bronze Shimmer from L'Oréal's Feria line. She sat on the simple navy-blue-cloth-upholstered Ektorp model sofa with her right leg crossed over her left. Seeing Weemer, her cheeks reddened slightly. She parted her full lips, and Weemer sensed that she was about to say something.

He was right.

"Hello, Steve," she said. Her voice was husky, with a slight accent, which many mistook for English, although Weemer *knew it was in fact a remnant of her upbringing in the Welsh coastal town of Fishguard, most famous for the fact that in 1797 it was the site of the last invasion of Britain, which was undertaken by a French attack force so incompetent even by French military standards that at one point twelve invaders surrendered to a forty-seven-year-old Fishguard woman, Jemima Nicholas, who was armed only with a pitchfork, an event commemorated by the Last Invasion Tapestry, which hangs today in Fishguard Town Hall.*[1]

"*Hello, Corinne,*" *he answered.*

Do you see how much *work* this is? It's already 377 words, and *virtually nothing has happened.* To get this novel off the ground and going somewhere, the writer will have to keep on cranking out descriptions for hundreds and hundreds of pages. It's brutal, slogging work, comparable to coal mining, but harder. You never hear coal miners complaining about Coal Miner's Block, wherein, try as they might, they simply can't bring themselves to mine another piece of coal. Whereas this kind of tragedy befalls novelists all the time, which is why so many of them are forced to quit working altogether and become university professors.

That's why screenwriting is such a good field for writers to get into. Screenwriters can skip most of the descriptions, because the movie viewers will see the action and setting for themselves

---

1. This is true.

and, if they are sitting behind me, comment upon it in a loud voice ("I have that exact same sofa! From Ikea! The Ektorp!"). If a screenwriter wants to write a scene in which some spectacular action takes place, he doesn't have to describe it in detail. He simply writes something like: "A savage monster clam rises out of the Potomac and eats the U.S. House of Representatives." Then he moves along in the plot, leaving it up to the computer-graphics nerds to figure out what that scene would actually *look* like.

So if a screenwriter were to write the 377-word scene above about Steve and Corinne, it would look like this:

EXT. DOORWAY

STEVE OPENS THE DOOR.

CORINNE
Hello, Steve.

STEVE
Hello, Corinne.

That's a grand total of twelve words, or a whopping 97 percent reduction in word count. Simply by eliminating description, the screenwriter can work his way through the entire plot in a single morning, leaving the afternoon free for screenwriter leisure activities such as drugs.

And yet, despite producing far fewer words than the novelist, the screenwriter often makes a LOT more money. Why? Because the average novel in the United States sells 173 copies, forty-eight of which are purchased by either the novelist or the novelist's mom. Whereas a screenplay has a chance to become a movie in which "Corinne" might be played by Angelina Jolie, and "Steve" might be played by Tom Cruise wearing special shoes to make him appear rangy, and it could make hundreds of millions of dollars and—even better—become a successful video game. A top screenwriter can earn tons of money, even if his movies tend to be, from an artistic and literary standpoint, monkey dung. That's why the rest of us writers look down on screenwriters and would give our excess kidneys to be one of them.

At least I always wanted to be one of them. My problem was that I could never figure out specifically what I had to do. Over the years I've gone to a bunch of writers' conferences, which are these gatherings where we writers form panels and explain to members of the reading public how hard writing is, after which there is a cocktail reception. From time to time at these events I've met people in the movie industry, and sometimes, after we've had a few cocktails, they'd say something along the lines of, "If you ever have any ideas for projects, let me know."

Each time this happened, I would get excited, because I knew I'd been given a golden opportunity to turn my movie ideas into money. The problem was, I didn't *have* any movie ideas. For almost all of my writing career, I've been a newspaper humor columnist, which means I have trained my brain to think of ideas that can be executed in short bursts between beers without heavy mental lifting. These ideas almost never involve deep cinematic themes. For me, the ideal topic is something like the one I used once for a Thanksgiving column, based on a newspaper story concerning the president of a company in Rancho Cucamonga, California, who proposed that the poultry industry could reduce meat contamination by Super Glue-ing turkey rectums shut.[2]

Now if you're a humor columnist trying to write a Thanksgiving column, a news story like this is a gift from God. It has all the elements you're looking for:

- Turkey rectums;
- Super Glue;
- Rancho Cucamonga;
- and most important of all,
- Turkey rectums.

But this kind of idea doesn't lend itself to the plot of a major motion picture. It is difficult to envision the following conver-

2. This is also true.

sation taking place between executives of a major movie studio:

> **FIRST EXECUTIVE:** Tell me about it.
>
> **SECOND EXECUTIVE:** It's a story of one man's courageous, lonely battle to expose the poultry industry's deadly secret—and the forces that will stop at nothing to bring him down.
>
> **FIRST EXECUTIVE:** What's it called?
>
> **SECOND EXECUTIVE:** *Rectums of Death.*
>
> **FIRST EXECUTIVE:** I like it.
>
> **SECOND EXECUTIVE:** Tom Cruise is on board, if we use short turkeys.

My other problem is that, even when I have a movie idea, I am not good at selling it. One time I was working on a youth novel called *Science Fair* with my friend and sometime writing partner Ridley Pearson. Ridley, who is more Hollywood-savvy than I am, managed to wangle us a conference call with some actual movie-studio people. The idea behind this call was that we would "pitch" our book idea as a possible movie. ("Pitching" is a Hollywood term for "trying to sell your project by acting like a low-cost prostitute, only with fewer scruples.") It was a golden opportunity, except for three problems:

First, we had written just two chapters of the book, so we

really didn't know what was going to happen in it. All we knew was that we intended it to be fun and wacky.

Second, Ridley and I are older guys born during the Civil War. This meant we had a generation gap, because the movie industry is very youth-oriented. The average age of movie-studio executives, at least the ones willing to talk to the likes of us, is approximately fourteen. But they are not the fun and wacky kind of fourteen-year-old. They are more along the lines of really young pension actuaries.

Third, since I had done most of the writing of what little of the book we had, Ridley and I decided that I would be the designated talker for our team, with Ridley providing backup. This turned out to be a large mistake. I have never "pitched" a movie. In fact, I am the world's worst salesperson. As a child, I never sold anything to anybody who was not one of my immediate parents. When I was supposed to be selling candy to my neighbors to raise money for Little League, my strategy was to walk very slowly to within thirty feet of a neighbor's door, then—this was my signature move—turn around and walk briskly away. The only way this sales strategy would have worked is if the neighbors happened to see me out the window and decided to chase me down, tackle me, and *demand* that I sell them some Little League candy. Even then I would probably have tried to talk them out of it.

So the conference call did not go well. I've managed to delete most of the specifics from my memory cells, but basically this is how it went:

> **MOVIE PEOPLE:** So tell us about *Science Fair.*
>
> **ME:** Well, it's . . . I mean, we haven't actually *written* it yet, but there's this science fair at this school, with these kids, and it gets really . . . wacky. Right, Ridley?
>
> **RIDLEY:** Yes! Wacky!
>
> **MOVIE PEOPLE:** Can you tell us some of the specific things that happen?
>
> **ME:** Sure! There's this . . . OK, there's this science fair, and these kids, um . . .
>
> *(There is an uncomfortable silence lasting perhaps forty seconds as the last bit of electrical activity in my brain flickers out.)*
>
> **RIDLEY** *(helping out):* It's a lot of fun!
>
> **ME:** Exactly! Fun!
>
> **MOVIE PEOPLE:** Maybe you could give us some specific plot points?
>
> **ME** *(frantically trying to remember something about the plot):* OK, there's, um . . . there's . . .
>
> *(Another hideously uncomfortable silence.)*
>
> **RIDLEY:** There's the guys with the cheese.
>
> **ME:** Right! The cheese!
>
> **MOVIE PEOPLE:** Cheese?
>
> **ME:** These guys, the bad guys, have this really powerful

cheese, which is, uh, it's one of the funny parts. Of the plot. The cheese.

RIDLEY: Fun!

You think I'm exaggerating, but if anything my pitch went worse. I was not connecting on any level. I was like a man trying to explain the Theory of Relativity without knowing anything about it, using only hand puppets. At one point the movie people mentioned that they were particularly interested in movie concepts that had main characters in four "quadrants"— male adult, female adult, male child, and female child. In an effort at a joke, I responded: "We have *six* quadrants! We have quadrants out the wazoo!" But the movie people did not seem to be amused. You could tell they took their quadrants seriously.

It will not surprise you to learn that Ridley and I failed to get a movie deal. But that was not the end of my Hollywood career, thanks to another friend of mine, Gene Weingarten. (That's right: I have *two* friends.) Gene has actually sold a screenplay, and he suggested that we should work together on one and become fabulously wealthy. That sounded like a solid business plan to me, so we agreed that he would fly down to Miami and stay at my house for a few days, during which we would have a movie idea, which we would then turn into a screenplay, which we would then sell in exchange for a large quantity of money.

I met Gene's flight at the Miami airport, and even though we had never collaborated on a screenplay before, within an hour—this is the kind of creative magic that can happen when two "pros" get together—we were able to locate my car in the parking garage. Like many aging Baby Boomers born before the discovery of quadrants, I've become forgetful, so I often have to locate my car by walking randomly around waving my remote control in front of me like a small magic wand, pressing it and listening for the answering beep. If for some reason you ever want to attract a bunch of Boomers, all you have to do is make a machine that beeps every few seconds and put it in the middle of a busy parking lot. You'll have Boomers swarming to it like ants to a Ding Dong.

Anyway, once we located my car, I figured we'd go to my house and try to have an idea, but Gene said, no, first we had to go to an office-supply store and buy a magnetic board. Really. Gene explained—remember, he was the guy who had actually sold a screenplay—that once we had a movie idea, we would break it down into scenes, and the correct way to organize these scenes was to write them on index cards, attach them to a board with magnets, and move them around until we had the right order. Gene insisted that this was how all the professional screenwriters did it.

So we went to Office Depot and bought a large white magnetic board, a bunch of index cards, and several dozen magnets.

Then we went to my house, set up the board, unpackaged the magnets and the index cards, made some coffee, settled into comfortable chairs, and prepared to have an idea.

That's where the process bogged down. We spent much of the first day using the magnets to make dirty words on the white-board. We did come up with some movie ideas. But none of them had that subtle, elusive quality that, for want of a better term, I will call "not being really stupid." I began to understand why so many movies—movies that were made at great expense, and with much effort—are so bad: It's really hard to come up with a good movie idea that somebody else hasn't already thought of. If you think of a truly original movie idea, one that has never been done, the odds are extremely high that it will suck.

What I think happens in Hollywood is, studio executives get constantly bombarded with horrible ideas, and this causes their brains to deteriorate. Eventually they reach the point where, if they hear an idea that sucks just a little bit less than all the others, they believe it's actually good. I say this because at some point, a conversation like the following must have actually taken place in a major Hollywood studio:

FIRST EXECUTIVE: Tell me about it.

SECOND EXECUTIVE: OK, a talking duck the size of a man gets transported from a duck planet to Cleveland on a laser beam. After working in a sauna, the duck gets into a fight with an evil being from another dimension who can recharge himself from a vehicle cigarette lighter. The duck finally wins and winds up staying on Earth as the manager of a rock band called Cherry Bomb.[3]

FIRST EXECUTIVE: I like it. Call them and make an offer.

SECOND EXECUTIVE: I can't remember how to work the phone.

A similar brain-deterioration problem afflicted Gene and me. There is no other explanation for the movie idea we came up with. You'll have to take my word for this: We are not complete idiots. We both have a lot of experience in the field of writing. We have both seen many movies. *We have both won Pulitzer Prizes.*[4] And yet, after three solid days of brainstorming, the movie concept that we settled on was:

Evil mutant superhuman chickens.

I swear I am not making this up. Our idea was that the chickens in an Iowa poultry plant, after years of being force-fed hormones and chemicals, have mutated and become powerful and highly intelligent, although they still look like regular

---

3. This is the actual plot of *Howard the Duck*, a 1986 movie made with a budget of $37 million.

4. And people wonder why the newspaper industry is in the toilet.

chickens. These chickens stage a revolt in their poultry plant and take an entire Iowa town hostage. Our hero, a young reporter named Mark, works at a supermarket tabloid newspaper patterned after the *Weekly World News*. He finds out about the chickens and writes a story about it, but nobody believes him because all the other stories in the paper are obvious fabrications like *Vampires on Supreme Court!* So he goes to the town and, with the help of an attractive female townsperson named Tami, saves the day by Super Glue-ing all the chickens' rectums shut.

I'm kidding about that last part. But I'm not kidding about the rest of the plot, which also involved the president of the United States, who goes to Iowa on a campaign trip and gets tangled up with Mark and Tami and the chickens in a fun and wacky way. Our working title was: *Chickens!*

Following the standard professional-screenwriter procedure, we wrote "CHICKENS" on an index card and attached it to the whiteboard with a magnet. To my knowledge, that was the last thing we ever did with the whiteboard. We spent the rest of our time typing on my computer, outlining the scenes we would include in our screenplay. I have saved the notes we made during this process. Here is a sampling:[5]

- *A race of super chickens. Very strong, very smart. They can talk.*

---

5. I am not making any of these notes up.

- *They hear a lot of hip-hop in the plant, and they really like it.*
- *Anybody who threatens them, they kill them.*
- *The owner of the factory—a real slimeball—is in cahoots— doesn't have to pay wages or salaries. Doesn't have to worry about unions.*
- *They need a few weeks to build a big enough supply of eggs—they're going to send eggs out all over the country in trucks.*
- *At some point, the chickens kill a PETA representative.*
- *Mark notices there are chickens on the street, giving him the eye.*
- *Goes to a bar—something weird—chicken there? Bartender scared?*
- *A plant worker tries to make a break—"I can't take any more!" The chickens take him down.*
- *Mark and Tami run outside, horrified. go to SHERIFF'S OFFICE. Look in the window—there sits the sheriff, surrounded by chickens.*
- *THE CAUCUSES ARE GOING ON.*
- *The president comes to town.*
- *Mark escapes the bad guys, pursued by bad guys and chickens.*
- *Gets into a debate or press conference.*
- *Informs the president.*
- *SOMEHOW IN THE COURSE OF HIS BEING DRAGGED AWAY SOMETHING HAPPENS WITH THE CHICKENS AND IT BECOMES CLEAR THAT HE'S TELLING THE TRUTH.*

- METHANE—*chickenshit raining down on Wolf Blitzer in Des Moines.*

I don't remember exactly what plot reason we had for that last note; maybe we were just responding to the universal human longing to see Wolf Blitzer inundated by chickenshit. All I know is, when Gene left Miami, we honestly, sincerely believed that this was the screenplay we were going to write.

Fortunately, as soon as we stopped exposing each other to bad ideas, our IQs started to rise. When we tried to actually write *Chickens!*, we quickly realized that we had come up with possibly the most ridiculous movie concept ever that was not part of the *Star Wars* franchise. So, using our restored brain function, we analyzed *Chickens!*, trying to pinpoint the problem. We decided it was: the chickens.

So we tweaked it. We kept the supermarket tabloid reporter and the presidential campaign, but we replaced the chickens with a political theme, and we wrote a screenplay that we called *Head of State*. We spent months working on it, sending scenes back and forth, writing and rewriting them. We got into heated arguments, because we had serious creative differences about certain elements of the story, by which I mean the size of the female characters' breasts. Gene felt they should all be small and perky; I did not. This dispute was both idiotic and irrelevant, because you don't put physical descriptions of characters in screenplays. But Gene, who for the record is insane, would re-gularly send me scenes that began like this:

INT. THE WHITE HOUSE

NATALIE ENTERS THE OVAL OFFICE WITH HER SMALL,
PERKY BREASTS.

I would feel compelled to revise this and send it back:

INT. THE WHITE HOUSE

NATALIE ENTERS THE OVAL OFFICE, FALLING FORWARD AS
GRAVITY ATTRACTS HER VAST BOSOMS.

We also worked on the actual plot, and we came up with what I still think was a pretty clever one, with numerous fun and wacky elements. To my knowledge, *Head of State* is the only screenplay ever written in which the president of the United States uses a nationally televised appearance to send a secret message by doing, in very slow motion, the Hokey Pokey.

When, at last, Gene and I were satisfied with *Head of State*, we sent it off to our agent in Los Angeles, a smart and savvy guy whom I will identify only as "Matt" so he can continue to have a career. Gene and I then sat back and prepared to consider the various incoming offers so we could decide which studio was the best "fit" for us in the sense of giving us the largest total number of dollars.

Except that no offers came in. I don't know what the problem was. Maybe we didn't have enough quadrants. Every few days Matt would send us an e-mail updating us on which studios had most recently passed on our screenplay. He tried to cheer us up by including tidbits of positive feedback ("This time it came back with very few vomit stains"). But as rejection followed rejection, we started to get the sinking feeling that our many hours of work had been for nothing, not to mention the cost of the magnetic board. After a while we both were convinced that the project had been a complete waste of time, and we pretty much forgot about it.

But sometimes, in real life as in the movies, there are happy endings. One day Gene and I got a brief e-mail from Matt: A studio had made an offer! He wanted to set up a conference call to explain it to us. I will never forget the moment when, after Gene and I were both on the line, Matt revealed the amount of money we were being offered. We were totally floored when he named the figure.

Fifty-eight dollars.

OK, technically it was more than that. But in Hollywood screenplay terms, the offer was the equivalent of $58. It was definitely less money than the average Hollywood movie production spends just on muffins.

Gene and I were deeply disappointed, and somewhat insulted. But in the end, we took the money, and for a very sound professional reason: We are whores. Also the contract said that if the studio decided that the screenplay needed to be rewritten, we would get first crack at it, and we would also be paid for that.

Several months after we sold our screenplay, some studio people called Gene and me to talk about the possibility of a rewrite. They were very nice. They said they really liked our screenplay, but wondered if we might want to consider "taking it in a different direction." Two of the directions they suggested—bear in mind, we had written a comedy about presidential politics—were:

- Making it about the National Football League.
- Making it into a musical.

This is kind of like telling Herman Melville you really like *Moby-Dick*, but you want to lose the whale. Not that I'm comparing *Head of State* to *Moby-Dick*. For one thing, *Head of State* has more fart jokes. But you see my point. We couldn't make it about the NFL without essentially dumping everything we'd written and starting over. And we definitely were not capable of turning it into a musical. I have written one reasonably successful song in my life, and it's about Tupperware. And compared to Gene, I am Mozart.

So we declined the offer to attempt a rewrite. As far as I know, nobody else has attempted one, either. I think *Head of State* has gone to that Big Screenplay Dumpster in the Sky. Although you never know; weird things can happen in the movie business. Maybe, in time, the studio will decide to revive our screenplay; maybe they'll hire somebody to rewrite it; and maybe it'll actually get the green light. So if, someday, you go to see a movie, and it turns out to be a musical about the NFL, remember whose idea that was: not ours.

But if it has superhuman chickens in it, I will be *pissed*.

24

The Ultimate Script

6 A.M.

The president, seen only in silhouette, sits at the head of a conference table. Seated around the table are the vice president, the Joint Chiefs of Staff, and various important-looking extras. The lighting is dim.

THE PRESIDENT

I've called you together because we have received intelligence concerning a serious threat that could . . . What is it, Mr. Vice President?

THE VICE PRESIDENT

Why is the lighting so dim?

THE PRESIDENT

For dramatic effect. You'll also notice that many characters in this show whisper for no good reason.

THE VICE PRESIDENT (PEERING AT THE PRESIDENT)

Wait a minute. You're a kangaroo.

THE PRESIDENT

Yes. The writers already did an African-American president and a woman president, so this season they were thinking, "Maybe a Jewish president?" And then they thought, "Nah, too unrealistic." So they went kangaroo.

THE VICE PRESIDENT

But is that even constitutional? And where do you go to the bathroom?

THE PRESIDENT

Nobody on this show goes to the bathroom.

THE VICE PRESIDENT

Touché.

THE PRESIDENT

As I was saying, we have received intelligence concerning a threat that could cause the deaths of millions of Americans.

THE VICE PRESIDENT

My God! What is it?

THE PRESIDENT

What is what?

THE VICE PRESIDENT

The threat.

THE PRESIDENT

I'll let the FBI director, played by a fading movie star such as William Hurt or Gene Hackman, answer that.

FBI DIRECTOR

We have reason to believe that a vaguely Middle Eastern terrorist organization has acquired a proton defrackulator.

THE VICE PRESIDENT

What's a proton defrackulator?

FBI DIRECTOR

We have no idea. But it sounds very bad.

THE PRESIDENT

Well, if these terrorists think I'm going to let them kill millions of Americans on my watch just because I have short, thumbless forelimbs, then they have another think coming. General, what do the Joint Chiefs recommend?

GENERAL

We recommend an immediate tactical nuclear missile strike against Boston.

THE PRESIDENT

Is that where the terrorists are?

GENERAL

No, we just hate Boston.

THE PRESIDENT

Fair enough. But we also need to do something about these terrorists.

CHIEF OF STAFF

If I may . . .

THE PRESIDENT

Aren't you one of the Baldwin brothers?

CHIEF OF STAFF

I believe so.

THE PRESIDENT

Go on.

CHIEF OF STAFF

There is only one man who can stop these terrorists, and that man is Jack Bauer.

THE PRESIDENT

Bauer . . . I know that name.

CHIEF OF STAFF

He's the main character.

THE PRESIDENT

Ah, right. But didn't he end the last season being arrested on trumped-up charges after he was framed by a shadowy cabal of powerful men?

CHIEF OF STAFF

That's how he ends every season.

THE PRESIDENT

So where is Bauer now?

CHIEF OF STAFF

He was imprisoned in a secret California prison facility.

THE PRESIDENT

Have him released.

CHIEF OF STAFF

He was also tortured.

THE PRESIDENT

Well, have a medical team . . .

CHIEF OF STAFF

Then he was decapitated and fed to boars.

THE PRESIDENT

Whoa.

CHIEF OF STAFF

Fortunately, he was trained for exactly that.

THE PRESIDENT

Are you saying that he could . . .

CHIEF OF STAFF

We won't know until after the commercial.

COMMERCIAL

SETTING: THE INFIRMARY OF A SECRET CALIFORNIA
PRISON

*Jack Bauer is sitting on an examination table. There are boar bites
all over his body and a bandage wrapped around his neck. A doctor
has just finished examining him.*

DOCTOR

You're going to experience some soreness from having
your head reattached to your body. I suggest you take it
easy for at least the next hour.

JACK

Give me your phone.

DOCTOR

If you need to make a call, there's a phone in the—

JACK

Dammit, there's NO TIME!

*Jack pulls a gun and shoots the doctor in the thigh. As the doctor
falls to the floor, Jack snatches his cell phone and dials a number.*

The scene shifts to an FBI office in Washington, D.C., where Chloe, sitting at her computer, answers the phone.

CHLOE

Hello?

JACK

Chloe, it's Jack.

CHLOE

Jack? I thought you were decapitated and consumed by boars.

JACK

Not anymore.

CHLOE

Thank God. I thought I wasn't getting any lines this season. Last year all I did was a PSA for Earth Day, while Janeane Garofalo got—

JACK

Dammit, Chloe, there's NO TIME. A terrorist cell is bringing in a proton defrackulator.

CHLOE

That sounds bad.

JACK

I need a map showing the port of entry for every international freight shipment in the past thirteen days weighing between fifty-two and sixty-three kilograms, overlaid with another grid showing the locations of all metropolitan areas with populations of twenty-eight thousand or more, overlaid with another grid showing prevailing wind direction and speed, overlaid with another grid showing the location of every odd-numbered Waffle House in North America.

CHLOE (TAPPING ON HER KEYBOARD)

I'm sending it now.

Jack looks at the cell-phone screen, which says: "DOWN-LOADING."

DOCTOR (WATCHING FROM THE FLOOR)

How are you doing that with my phone? I can't even get a signal in here.

Jack, without taking his eyes off the phone, shoots the doctor in the other thigh to silence him. The phone is now displaying a detailed map with many symbols, including a blinking red dot over Washington, D.C.

JACK

Looks like they're bringing the defrackulator into the Washington area.

CHLOE

That makes sense. All the other main characters are here.

JACK (STEPPING OVER THE DOCTOR AND HEADING FOR THE EXIT)

I'll need transport.

CHLOE (TAPPING)

I'll send a helicopter.

Jack runs outside. A helicopter immediately appears overhead.

JACK

OK, I see it.

CHLOE

What?

JACK

Sorry. I mean I have a visual on it. Have the FBI set up

a perimeter around Washington, Maryland, and Virginia. Don't let anybody in or out. Shut down the shipping lanes and set up satellite surveillance to detect anybody on the Eastern Seaboard who looks vaguely Middle Eastern.

CHLOE (TAPPING)

I'm on it.

Jack runs to the helicopter. The pilot opens the door. Jack climbs in. The pilot gestures for Jack to put on his seat belt. Jack shouts something, shoots the pilot in the thigh, throws him out of the chopper, grabs the controls, and takes off.

COMMERCIAL

SETTING: A SEAPORT

Two vaguely Middle-Eastern-looking terrorists are watching as a crane lowers a wooden crate from a freighter to the pier. Stenciled on the side of the crate are the words "HARMLESS MACHINE PARTS."

FIRST TERRORIST

Once the proton defrackulator is loaded into the van, we'll take it to our secret hideout in Washington.

SECOND TERRORIST

Then we will activate it and carry out the plan to kill millions of Americans.

FIRST TERRORIST

You should roll your "r"s, so our accents sound more alike.

The two men watch as dockworkers finish loading the crate into a white van. The first man pulls out a cell phone and dials a number.

FIRST TERRORIST (INTO PHONE)

I have the floral centerpiece and will deliver it to the wedding reception. (He ends the call.)

SECOND TERRORIST

Was that a coded message to the terrorist mastermind?

FIRST TERRORIST

No, that was my brother-in-law, the florist. I'm helping him out with a wedding.

SECOND TERRORIST

Let's get going, then. Those millions of Americans aren't going to kill themselves!

The two men enjoy a vaguely Middle Eastern laugh, then shoot the dockworkers, get into the van, and drive away.

COMMERCIAL

SETTING: INSIDE THE HELICOPTER

Jack is at the controls. The phone he took from the doctor rings. He plugs a Bluetooth headset into his ear.

JACK

Jack Bauer.

CHLOE

Jack, we just got satellite recon video showing unusual activity at the Chevy Chase seaport.

JACK

What kind of unusual activity?

CHLOE

Two men took possession of a crate exactly the size of a proton defrackulator, loaded it into a van, and took off. Also they shot all the dockworkers.

JACK

Hmm. Were they swarthy?

CHLOE (TAPPING)

I'm uploading a photo.

JACK (LOOKING AT PHONE)

Those are terrorists, all right. Do you have a visual on the van?

CHLOE (TAPPING)

Yes.

JACK

What?

CHLOE

Sorry. I mean, affirmative. The van stopped at a wedding reception to deliver a floral centerpiece.

JACK

What kind?

CHLOE (TAPPING)

Cymbidium orchids in a bed of asparagus leaves accented with wisps of bear grass.

JACK

Bear grass?

CHLOE (TAPPING)

Latin name *Xerophyllum tenax*.

JACK

Copy that. Where's the van now?

CHLOE

It's heading toward the Department of Commerce building in downtown Washington on Old Plankton Road.

JACK

Keep me posted. I'm landing at the White House now.

The chopper lands on the White House lawn. Jack jumps out, shoots a Marine attempting to salute him, and strides into the White House. An instant later he enters the Situation Room.

THE PRESIDENT

Mr. Bauer, thank you for . . . Whoa, are those boar bites?

JACK

There was also an ocelot. I'll be fine.

THE PRESIDENT

Ouch. Anyway, thank you for coming from California in eight minutes.

THE VICE PRESIDENT

I say we arrest him on trumped-up charges for crimes he did not commit.

THE PRESIDENT

Not yet, you moron. Jack, what do you know about the plot?

JACK

The terrorists brought the proton defrackulator in through the Chevy Chase seaport and are heading into Washington on Old Plankton Road.

FBI DIRECTOR

Wait a minute. There is no "Chevy Chase seaport," and no "Old Plankton Road."

THE PRESIDENT

If you think that with millions of American lives at stake I'm going to sit here and listen to your legalistic nitpicking just because once a year after thirty-one to thirty-six days of gestation I give birth to a blind hairless infant the size of a lima bean and then nurse it to maturity from a teat in my pouch, then you have another think coming. General, what do the Joint Chiefs recommend?

GENERAL
We—

Jack shoots the general in the thigh.

JACK
There's no time for that. I'll need a tactical assault team of extras headed by an attractive woman.

THE PRESIDENT
Done.

JACK
Also I may have to blow up the Department of Commerce. Apparently it's a terrorist hideout.

THE PRESIDENT
I wondered what they did in there.

Jack strides out. For a moment the Situation Room is silent.

THE VICE PRESIDENT

Wait . . . you're a female kangaroo?

COMMERCIAL

SETTING: DOWNTOWN WASHINGTON, D.C.

Jack lands the helicopter outside the Department of Commerce Building. As he climbs out, an attractive black-clad woman approaches. Jack shoots her.

WOMAN (CLUTCHING HER THIGH)

Wait! FBI!

JACK

Sorry.

WOMAN

It's just a bullet wound; it'll heal in a few minutes. I'm Faye Baker, your romantic interest.

JACK

Be advised that I have a brooding personality and never allow anyone to get too close.

FAYE

Is that because of the lonely burden you bear?

JACK

Also I haven't pooped in nine years. Have you established a totally ineffective perimeter?

FAYE

Of course.

JACK (SPEAKING INTO PHONE)

Chloe, I need the building schematics now.

CHLOE (TAPPING)

Uploading.

JACK (LOOKING AT PHONE)

These are pictures of you naked.

CHLOE

Whoops.

JACK

Is that a llama?

CHLOE (TAPPING FURIOUSLY)

Here are the schematics.

JACK (FROWNING AT PHONE)

According to these, we can enter the building by . . . the door.

CHLOE (TAPPING)

Jack, there's something else.

JACK

What is it?

CHLOE

I just ran a cross-modulated algorithm sequentialization series on the HEPCOM database, and for shocking-plot-twist reasons that make no logical sense, which is why I'm talking really fast and using random technical-sounding buzzwords, your son is in that building.

JACK

I have a son?

CHLOE

Apparently this season you do.

JACK

Copy that. TO FAYE: We need to get to the proton de-frackulator before the terrorists activate it at the top of the hour.

FAYE

But what about your son?

JACK (BROODING)

I don't want to talk about it.

FAYE

Don't shut me out, Jack.

JACK

Dammit, Faye, there's NO TIME.

Jack runs into the building, followed by Faye and her team. They are met in the lobby by a hail of bullets. Many extras go down. Jack pulls a pistol and fires approximately eight hundred shots, each of which kills an enemy gunman. But more gunmen keep appearing. Jack and Faye crouch behind a lamp. Tens of thousands of bullets ricochet around them.

JACK (SHOUTING INTO BLUETOOTH HEADSET)

Chloe, we're pinned down by hostiles in the Department of Commerce!

CHLOE

I wondered what they did in there.

JACK (SHOUTING)

I need the location of the defrackulator!

CHLOE (TAPPING)

It's in the basement, next to the National Aquarium.

JACK

Why is the National Aquarium in the Commerce Department Building?

CHLOE (TAPPING)

Nobody knows. Jack, there's something else. They've put your son into the octopus tank.

JACK

Copy that. Faye, cover me. I'm going down there.

FAYE

I love you, Jack.

JACK

Copy that.

Through a blizzard of bullets, Jack runs across the lobby, killing people en route. He runs into an elevator, which contains fourteen hostile gunmen. The door closes. As the elevator descends, Jack and the gunmen engage in a fierce gunfight, during which he kills them all. The door opens and Jack stumbles out of the elevator into the basement.

JACK (SHOUTING INTO HEADSET)

Which way?

CHLOE (TAPPING)

To the right! Hurry, Jack! We're almost at the top of the hour!

Jack runs to his right. Ahead is the aquarium tank; inside it, in the grasp of an octopus, is a young man, played by Keanu Reeves. Next to the tank is one of the terrorists, doing something to what looks like a large espresso machine.

JACK (AIMING GUN)

Step away from the defrackulator NOW!

TERRORIST

You're too late, Bauer!

KEANU REEVES

Dad! Help!

As Jack looks toward his son, Chloe's voice shouts in his earpiece.

CHLOE

Jack! Look out behind you!

Jack starts to turn, but he's too late. The second terrorist leaps from a hallway with a machete and whacks Jack's head off.

CHLOE

Jack! Are you all right?

JACK'S HEAD (ON FLOOR)

I'll be fine.

FIRST TERRORIST (PUSHING A BUTTON)

The proton defrackulator has been activated!

JACK'S HEAD

What does it do, anyway?

FIRST TERRORIST

We actually don't know. But we assume it's bad.

The camera zooms in on the proton defrackulator to reveal a digital timer counting down . . . 15 . . . 14 . . . 13 . . .

KEANU REEVES

Dad! A tentacle is grasping my privates!
Clock: 6:59:59

THE SCREEN GOES DARK

COMMERCIAL

JACK BAUER'S VOICE
Following are scenes from next week's *24*.

SETTING: THE WHITE HOUSE SITUATION ROOM

CHIEF OF STAFF
Madam President, Newark is gone.

THE PRESIDENT
Newark, New Jersey, or Newark, Delaware?

CHIEF OF STAFF
What difference does it make?

THE PRESIDENT
Good point!

Everybody enjoys a hearty laugh.

QUICK CUT TO: A DIMLY LIT ROOM

Jack, his head hastily reattached to his body with blood-soaked duct tape, stands over a shadowy figure in a chair. Jack is hold-

ing a power drill in one hand and a bottle of Tabasco sauce in the
other.

JACK

You're going to talk, do you understand? I'm going to make you talk.

The camera slowly pans around to reveal that the figure in the chair is: the octopus.

QUICK CUT TO: THE SECRET HEADQUARTERS OF THE SHADOWY CABAL THAT RUNS EVERYTHING

Two shadowy cabal members are smoking cigars in a dimly lit room.

FIRST CABAL MEMBER

We need to have Bauer arrested on trumped-up charges again before he finds out what we're really planning, which will have nothing whatsoever to do with anything that has happened so far.

SECOND CABAL MEMBER

What are we really planning?

FIRST CABAL MEMBER

Those episodes aren't written yet.

SECOND CABAL MEMBER

Ow!

FIRST CABAL MEMBER

What is it?

SECOND CABAL MEMBER

I put my cigar out on my hand.

FIRST CABAL MEMBER

Damn this dim lighting.

END OF EPISODE ONE

The Full Coward Package

Recently I went shopping for two items:

1. A jockstrap.
2. A bag of frozen peas.

These items may seem unrelated to you. But certain men, upon reading that list, will wince when they recognize these as the items that you need when you get a . . .

(*Cue scary font*)

Vasectomy

The frozen peas are to minimize the swelling in your personal manliness zone. The jockstrap is to keep you from dangling. After a vasectomy—trust me—you do *not* want to dangle.

Not to sound boastful, but: I went with a size large jockstrap. It brought back vivid memories of gym class at Pleasantville High School, where we male students were required to wear jockstraps so that our larger classmates could use us as human slingshots by grabbing our elastic strap from behind, pulling it back several feet, and releasing it to cause the Twang of Pain.

Shopping for peas was trickier, because the supermarket had such a large selection.

"These are good," said my wife, holding a bag of Green Giant Steamers Sweet Peas, a premium brand.

"I'm not going to *eat* them," I said. "I'm going to put them on my b***s."[1]

In the end I went with the Birds Eye Spring Garden Peas. I recommend them, if you're a man who is getting a vasectomy. But before you take this major step, you should get answers to some important medical questions, starting with: Are you *insane*?

No, really, you should have some information, such as: What, exactly, happens to you in a vasectomy? I can answer this question, thanks to a helpful pamphlet I got from my urologist, titled

1. Balls.

VASECTOMY: *Permanent Birth Control for Men*, which I read as carefully as I could, considering that I had my eyes closed.

Based on this research, I would say that the best way to understand a vasectomy is to compare human reproduction to the New York City transit system, with Manhattan as the penis. In normal reproduction, the sperm cells originate in the testicles, represented by Brooklyn and Queens, then proceed via the vas deferens, represented by the Brooklyn Bridge and Queens-Midtown Tunnel, to Manhattan, where they join up with the seminal fluid, manufactured by the seminal vesicles and the prostate gland, represented by Staten Island. The sperm cells then travel through a long tube called the urethra, represented by the IRT Broadway Local line, exiting Manhattan at the tip and being deposited in the female vagina, represented by Van Cortlandt Park in the Bronx.

In a vasectomy, the doctor severs the conduits from Brooklyn and Queens, leaving the sperm cells trapped in the outer boroughs, where they eventually die because there are no decent nightclubs. Vasectomy is a safe, effective, and reliable procedure, and there is absolutely no reason to be afraid of it, except that

They cut a hole in your scrotum.

Medically, this is no big deal. It's an outpatient procedure. When it's done, you simply get up and walk out. Recovery takes just a couple of days. Most men experience only minor discomfort. Nevertheless, if you're a man considering taking this step, you need to reflect upon the fact that if you get a vasectomy,

They are going to cut a hole IN YOUR SCROTUM.

I can hear you veteran women readers going: "You think that's bad? A little *hole*? Until you've had a baby you have NO IDEA what it means to experience discomfort in the privates."

OK, on behalf of men, I will stipulate to you women that childbirth is not only very painful, but also a clear violation of the laws of physics. But you have to understand that we men have a very special relationship with our testicles. They are the most sensitive and vulnerable organs we have, and we are very protective of them because of vivid memories of the various times when we took a hard shot to the cubits and spent several excruciating minutes writhing on the ground, curled up like jumbo shrimp, wishing that a medical caregiver would come along and shoot us in the head.

If you've ever watched a soccer match, you've probably noticed that, during a penalty kick, the defenders—who stand only ten yards away from the guy who's about to kick the ball really hard—use both of their hands to protect their groins. They do not spare so much as a single hand to protect their heads. These men are clearly saying that, if forced to decide which is their *most* vital organ, they are not choosing their brains.

So with all due respect to women: You cannot really appreciate the electric shock of fear that shoots through a man when he contemplates the prospect of allowing somebody to take a sharp implement and

CUT A FREAKING HOLE IN. HIS. SCROTUM.

Nevertheless, a lot of guys get it done, because they have reached a stage in their lives when they have the wisdom, the maturity, and the perspective necessary to understand that if they do *not* get a vasectomy, their wives will never ever stop bringing it up. You may be one of these guys. To determine if you're a vasectomy candidate, ask yourself:

- Do you wish to be rendered permanently incapable of fathering children?
- Would you enjoy spending several days watching TV with a bag of frozen peas in your crotch?

If you answered "yes" to both questions, you should make an appointment to see a urologist. What you should NOT do—this is very important—is go on the Internet and read the vasectomy message boards, because you will see anecdotes like this:

One of my co-workers got a vasectomy and his sperm backed up and, long story short, two weeks later his scrotum exploded during his performance review.

And:

My brother-in-law was getting a vasectomy and right after the doctor made the incision there was an earthquake and the operating table shook so hard that both his testicles fell out and rolled across the floor and into the waiting room, where a blind patient was waiting with his seeing-eye dog, which . . .

Pay no attention to these hearsay anecdotes. Your vasectomy will be a walk in the park, although for a day or two it will be the walk of the late Walter Brennan as Grandpappy Amos McCoy. But the procedure itself will be nothing, especially if you do it the way I did it; namely, unconscious.

I'm a big believer in anesthesia. I think it should be used for every medical procedure, including routine physicals. I'd like to be knocked out while I was still in the doctor's waiting room and not regain consciousness until everything is over, ideally in my car, with no memory whatsoever of what happened.

I'd also like to see anesthesia used in non-medical settings. Like, if for some reason you had to attend the opera, there would be an anesthesiologist in the lobby, next to the candy stand. He'd knock you out and special brawny ushers would drag you to your seat and leave you there, drooling into your lap, until it was over. I think there should also be anesthesiologists on hand for meetings, ballet recitals, banquets, charity galas, and movies based on books that my wife likes (fatal diseases; no punching).

But the point is that you definitely want anesthesia for your vasectomy. Tell your doctor you want the Full Coward Package. Tell him you don't necessarily want to wake up during the same *month* as your procedure. That's what I did. I was totally out for the whole thing, and it worked out fine, aside from the video that later appeared on YouTube featuring a close-up of my privates dressed up in a tiny Elvis outfit.

I'm kidding, of course! It was a large Elvis outfit.

No, *seriously*: Nothing happened. I went home with my jockstrap and my peas, and in a few days I was able to resume my regular exercise regimen of mostly sitting around. So if you've been thinking about getting a vasectomy, my sincere advice to you is: Do *not* read this essay. You're welcome.

The Health-Care Crisis

Wash Your Hands After Reading This

When we analyze the American health-care system, we see that the most important questions facing us, as a nation, are:

- How should we pay for health care?
- Who should make our health-care decisions?
- What is this weird little skin thing on my right forefinger that won't go away?

I think we can all agree that our highest priority, as a nation, is my weird forefinger thing. So far, I've been following the standard course of treatment recommended for diseases in general by the American Academy of Physicians with Framed Latin Diplomas, namely, picking fretfully at the affected area. But after months of fretful picking without any forefinger improvement, I'm thinking of breaking down and going to see the skin doctor.

I'm reluctant to go see any doctor, but especially my skin doctor. I went to her a few years ago when I contracted a rare and very serious disease consisting of cancer combined with smallpox, leprosy, cholera, heart failure, and the bubonic plague. At least that was my diagnosis based on the symptoms, which consisted of: pain. But it turned out, according to my skin doctor, that what I actually had was "shingles," a disease that gets its name from the fact that it is transmitted by roofers, which, as a resident of Florida, I am exposed to constantly.

The skin doctor gave me medicine for my shingles, but she also told me that I should (1) eat a lot of broccoli, and (2) not drink alcohol. I asked her if she meant I should not drink alcohol while I had shingles, and she said, no, her medical opinion was that people in general should never, ever drink any alcohol. At all.

Well, I may not have a framed Latin diploma, but I know crazy talk when I hear it. Alcohol has been an important part of the human diet for thousands of years. The Bible is filled with references to people drinking alcohol, such as this quotation from the Book of Effusions, Chapter Eight, Verse Six, Row 7:

And yea, they did smite the Phalanges, and to celebrate they held-eth a party and they dranketh some alcohol in the form of wine, and it was good. So they also diddeth some shooters. Then they saideth, "Hey, let us doeth some more smiting."

Oh, I'm not saying that alcohol is perfect. It has caused its share of problems. Russia is only one example. But throughout history, alcohol has shown that, used correctly, it can be a powerful force for good. I personally have won many crucial arguments at parties because alcohol gave me the conviction to keep arguing until my opponent had no choice but to leave, even if he or she was the host. And consider this: If there were no alcohol, there would be no straight white men dancing at weddings. There also would be no such sport as "luge." And virtually none of the scientific discoveries concerning what happens when you launch bottle rockets from a set of human buttocks would ever have been made. Is that the kind of world you want to live in? Me neither.

I have, however, been eating more broccoli.

But getting back to the American health-care situation: It is bad. Consider the following disturbing facts:

- FACT: American health care is a $2.5-trillion-per-year industry.
- FACT: And yet it cannot make a hospital gown that completely covers your ass.
- FACT: This year, 253 million Americans will seek emergency medical treatment.
- FACT: If you have to go to the Emergency Room, ALL of these Americans will be waiting in line ahead of you.
- FACT: And the waiting area will have a TV playing episodes of *Judge Judy* at the volume of the Daytona 500.

- FACT: On average, Canadians live 1.7 years longer than Americans.
- FACT: But because they live in Canada, it feels more like twelve years.
- FACT: And because they use the metric system, this is actually the equivalent of 15.3 American years.
- FACT: The male hammerhead bat, which attracts females by making a honking sound, has a larynx that takes up *more than half of its body.*

Clearly, we have a crisis on our hands. The question is: What should we do about it? To answer that question, we must first figure out how we got into this mess in the first place. So let's review:

The History of Medical Care

In prehistoric times, people believed that sickness was caused by angry spirits invading a person's body. To get rid of these spirits, sick people went to see primitive medical specialists called "shamans,"[1] who would "cure" them by sacrificing a goat. Of course this was all a bunch of superstitious nonsense. We now know, thanks to modern medical science, that the shaman was

---

1. Or, in modern parlance, "chiropractors."

actually making things *worse*, because when he sacrificed the goat he released the *goat's* spirit, which was (Who can blame it?) *really* angry, and which would proceed to invade some totally innocent human. Scientists now believe this is what happened to Nick Nolte.

The first big breakthrough in medical knowledge was made by the ancient Egyptians, who discovered that the human body contained organs such as the pancreas, and if a person became sick, and you took out one or more of these organs, the person would get better. Or not. But either way you could charge the person, or his heirs, money. This was the beginning of surgery.

The next big players in medicine were the ancient Greeks, who believed that disease was caused by an imbalance of the body's four "humours": blood, bile, phlegm, and sarcasm. This made for some really disgusting treatments, especially if you were diagnosed as being phlegm-deficient, in which case you had to have a transfusion from a compatible loogie donor.

The greatest Greek physician of all was Hippocrates, who is often called "the father of modern medicine" because he invented the concept that remains the foundation of all medical care as we know it today: the receptionist. Prior to this invention, when patients came to see the doctor, the doctor had to actually *see* them, which as you can imagine took up a lot of his valuable time because they were always nattering on and on about being sick. But all of a sudden, thanks to Hippocrates, incoming patients could be intercepted by a receptionist, who would (1) tell them to take a seat, and then (2) avoid making eye contact with them for the rest of the afternoon. This breakthrough meant that a single doctor could schedule as many as 375 appointments per hour, which is the system we still use today.

After the ancient Greeks came the ancient Romans, who advanced the cause of medicine by inventing sewers, running water,[2] and of course Latin, without which modern diplomas would not be incomprehensible.

This was followed by the Middle Ages, during which medical care consisted of putting dress pants on the corpses.

Then, in 1676, came one of the most important medical breakthroughs of all. A Dutch scientist named Antonie van

---

2. That's right: Before the Romans, *water stood still.*

Leeuwenhoek, who had developed an improved method for making optical lenses, was peering through a microscope at a drop of his saliva, when he made an astounding discovery: the letters in "Antonie van Leeuwenhoek" could be rearranged to spell "Look, Nun, at Weenie Heaven!"[3]

Unfortunately, Antonie didn't speak English, so he didn't realize how entertaining this was. Instead he went back to looking through his microscope, and he made another astounding discovery: Some very tiny things were moving around in his saliva. Upon peering closer, he realized that what he was seeing were actually living creatures—but very strange-looking creatures, unlike anything ever seen before:

3. Also: "Eel-toe union? Wank Heaven!"

These creatures, of course, were bacteria, which are one-celled animals that thrive in places such as nasal passages, armpits, public restrooms, and yogurt. When van Leeuwenhoek publicized his discovery, medical scientists realized that these tiny organisms in our bodies were the cause of many diseases. This in turn led them to the conclusion that the logical way to treat these diseases was to . . . *sacrifice a goat*. So there was still a long way to go.

By the 1800s, animal sacrifice had been largely discredited as a medical procedure; today it is rarely used outside of Miami. But nineteenth-century medical care was still quite primitive by modern standards. Hospital patients were routinely tied to their beds with leather restraints and told to bite down on pieces of wood while surgeons used unsterilized saws to cut off their arms or legs. And these patients were being treated for *ear infections*. You don't want to know what happened to people with hemorrhoids.

Things really started to improve in 1895 when German physicist Wilhelm Roentgen, while doing some laboratory experiments to see if anything came after W-rays, discovered X-rays. This made it possible for the first time for doctors to look inside living human beings and spot problems such as cancerous tumors, which, as it turned out, were caused by exposure to X-rays. So this invention came along just in the nick of time.

The twentieth century saw a tremendous improvement in the quality of medical care thanks to such advances as—to name just a few—penicillin, the artificial heart, liposuction, the little hammer that the doctor uses to hit your knee, the answering service, the six-year-old *Woman's Day* magazines for patients to read in the waiting room, the deductible, the artificial wart, the sphincter transplant, and the consumer-safe pill bottle that the consumer cannot open without power tools.

Today, in the twenty-first century, America is the most medically advanced nation on Earth. And yet many Americans are unhappy with our current health-care system. To understand why, we must first type a subheading that says:

The Current American Health-Care System

The journey through the American health-care system typically begins when a typical American, whom we will call Mary,[4] is watching television and sees a commercial for a prescription drug with a name that sounds like a *Star Wars* planet, such as "Lipitor" or "Zoloft." This commercial shows trained actors pretending to be regular humans just like Mary, ruefully telling the camera how foolish they feel because they failed to ask their doctor about the prescription drug—we'll call it "Endor"[5]—that

4. Not her real name.
5. This actually *is* the name of a *Star Wars* planet; it's the one with the Ewoks, the creatures that look like spear-carrying Yorkshire terriers. Endor should not be taken by pregnant women, or women who know any other women who might be, or might someday become, pregnant.

paid millions of dollars to make the commercial. The commercial does not make it entirely clear what Endor does, but it *is* clear that if you don't ask your doctor about it, you have the IQ of spinach.

At the end of the commercial, an announcer warns Mary about the possible side effects of Endor, including (but not limited to) headache, nausea, spontaneous combustion of the eyeballs, and death of the patient and the patient's entire extended family. But Mary isn't paying attention to the announcer. She's thinking that, although she feels perfectly healthy, she doesn't want to be the kind of idiot loser who fails to ask her doctor about Endor.

So Mary calls her doctor's office and speaks to a semi-medical professional who tells her that the doctor will be able to see her in . . . (*tapping of computer keys*) . . . three months. Mary puts this on her calendar, but there's really no need for a reminder, because over the next three months she will see the Endor commercial 783 more times. She reaches the point, emotionally, where pretty much all she wants to do in life is ask her doctor about Endor.

On the appointed day, Mary goes to her doctor's office, where a semi-medical professional conducts a thorough examination of Mary's health-insurance ID card, then instructs her to take a seat. She is left to season in the waiting room with three or four dozen other patients (several clearly deceased) and old *Woman's Day* magazines for a period ranging from one to four hours, after which another semi-medical professional calls her name.

Now, finally, after all the waiting and the worry, Mary will have the opportunity to . . . be weighed. Weighing patients is an ancient medical tradition, dating back to the shamans, who believed that a person's weight indicated how large an evil spirit was inhabiting his body. The semi-medical professional doesn't even bother writing Mary's weight down.

Mary is then ushered into a small, stark examination room furnished with a plastic chair, a paper-covered examination table, and a large, detailed color diagram of the human endocrine system to remind Mary that there are many important things about medicine that a layperson like herself cannot hope to understand. The semi-medical professional leaves, closing the door. Mary sits there, alone, looking at the diagram. The minutes tick past. Fifteen minutes. Thirty minutes. Mary begins to wonder if they have forgotten about her. She also becomes increasingly convinced that something is wrong—very wrong—with her endocrine system.

Then, just when she's about to give up hope of ever receiving medical care, she hears footsteps in the hallway. Suddenly, the door opens, and in steps: another semi-medical professional. She's there to make sure Mary has not died of malnutrition, and to let her know that the doctor will be with her shortly. This is accurate: The doctor will be with her *very* shortly, because he has 374 other patients to see during that hour, which means he has budgeted 9.6 seconds total for Mary, including pleasantries.

When, at last, the doctor appears, he moves at the speed of an HBO vampire. He emits a .016-second pleasantry burst and immediately starts writing things down. Mary has no idea what he is writing, but she realizes that if she doesn't ask her question quickly, the doctor will be gone. So she blurts it out.

"I'm wondering if I need Endor," she says.

"I'll schedule some tests," the doctor replies, writing furiously. And then, with another pleasantry (truncated to .009 seconds, as the doctor is running late) he is gone, leaving no trace of his visit except the gentle rustling of the endocrine-system chart on the wall.

What Mary doesn't know is that the doctor, focusing on completing his paperwork, heard her incorrectly; instead of "I'm wondering if I need Endor," the doctor thought she said, "I'm wondering if my feet are tender." So he has ordered X-rays of Mary's feet, and—to protect himself from a potential lawsuit being filed by the medical-malpractice attorneys who flock around his building— orders a full blood workup, urinalysis, bone-density scan, electrocardiogram, MRI, full-body CAT scan, several biopsies, and a barium enema.

Mary, following the directions on a piece of paper handed to her by a semi-medical professional, goes to a medical laboratory, where needle-wielding technicians in medical attire systematically drain the bulk of her bodily fluids. She then goes home to wait, and fret. Several days later, she gets a call from a worker at her doctor's office, saying the doctor wishes to speak with her. A few moments later, or possibly forty-five minutes later, the doctor comes on the line personally. He tells Mary that he has good news and bad news. The good news is, there appears to be nothing wrong with Mary's feet.

My feet? thinks Mary, but before she can say anything, the doctor springs the bad news: One of the tests has turned up a troubling result—a small, strange-looking spot showed up on one of the test scans:

The doctor assures Mary that the spot could very well be nothing. In fact, it *is* nothing; it was caused when a lab technician, while processing Mary's images, sneezed up a globule of mayonnaise from the tuna sub he had for lunch. But the doctor doesn't know this, and he is not about to take any chances with the spot, because looking out his office window, he can see a flock of medical-malpractice attorneys watching him from their perches in a tree across the street. So he tells Mary he is sending her to a specialist for additional tests.

A few days later Mary goes to the specialist's office, where, after the standard seasoning and weighing, she is ushered to an examination room containing a realistic full-sized model of the human spine that looks like a huge prehistoric insect. She stares nervously at this until the specialist materializes. In his allotted seconds with Mary, he can't find anything that might have caused the spot, but to be on the safe side, he orders Mary back to the lab for additional tests involving the removal of whatever bodily fluids Mary may have left. Several days later, the specialist gets the results. They do not shed any light on Mary's spot. The specialist is on the verge of telling Mary it was probably nothing when he hears the distinctive sound of restless attorneys scuffing their wingtip shoes on his office roof. So he decides that, rather than take any chances, he will refer Mary to another specialist.

The process repeats itself, again and again. Mary becomes a human hot potato, passed from specialist to specialist, each of them sending Mary back to the laboratory for more tests because none of them wants to have to explain to a jury, under questioning from a malpractice attorney, why he or she was the only doctor in this chain of specialists who failed to see the need to subject Mary to more medical care.

Mary is now a psychological and physical wreck from wondering what is wrong with her, not to mention giving out more fluid samples than a Napa Valley winery. Also she's not getting much sleep, because every day the postal person wheezes up to her mailbox and deposits a large bale of insurance-company statements, which look like this:

EXPLANATION OF BENEFITS

HealthLifeCorp
Formerly LifeHealth Corp
Formerly United Tongue Depressor

Medical Provider Name	Date of Service	Procedure Code	Total Charge	Adjusted Gross Basis	Net Residual Accrued Debenture	Postage and Gratuities	Last Number for Now
Himple	03/13/10	385345-803	$635.79	523.98	43.72	243.09	324.56
Kornfutter	03/16/10	589458320b	1,436.89	54.67	3,267.45	98.48	7,968.45
Ferb	03/22/10	7664735&54	147,983.25	5,779.09	9,237.45	32,286.16	329,986.03

Mary reads these statements with no more comprehension than a tree frog pondering the space shuttle. She wonders: What do these numbers mean? Is she supposed to pay any of the amounts shown? Which ones? To whom? What if she *can't* pay?

Mary becomes increasingly depressed, and finally decides to seek the help of a psychiatrist. The psychiatrist, after carefully evaluating Mary's condition to determine that her health insurance includes psychiatric coverage, prescribes a tranquilizer called Coruscant.[6] Unfortunately, this drug causes Mary to experience a rare but serious side effect in the form of severe tenderness of the feet.

<hr />

6. As featured in *Episode III: Revenge of the Sith*.

Mary starts skipping work. She spends most of her days sitting in her Barcalounger, surrounded by piles of benefit explanations, watching TV. Thirty to forty times per day she is exposed to a locally produced commercial for a team of lawyers who have dark suits, a complete set of legal-looking books lined up on professional bookshelves, and a burning desire to fight for the legal rights of whoever is watching daytime television.

Finally Mary decides that the fighting attorneys are talking to *her*. She calls the number on the screen and makes an appointment. Within hours she has been fitted with orthopedic shoes, crutches, a wheelchair, and a neck brace, and she is the plaintiff in a lawsuit naming, as defendants, every doctor she has ever seen, every drug she has ever taken, every medical lab she has ever been tested by, and the publishers of *Woman's Day*.

Mary ultimately receives an out-of-court settlement of $18,000. After the team of fighting lawyers take their fee and deduct their expenses—orthopedic shoes are *not* cheap—Mary is left with $1,263.47. She is now unemployed, uninsured, and broke, with unpaid medical bills approaching $500,000. She feels sicker than ever, but is terrified about what might happen to her if she gets any more professional health care. She has started to explore alternative healing practices. When we see her last, she has contacted a healing practitioner who claims to have obtained excellent results in cases just like Mary's. All the practitioner needs is for Mary to bring him $50 cash.

And a live goat.

Now I know what you're saying. You're saying: "Dave, you have painted a distorted and inaccurate picture of the American health-care system. Not all patients wind up being as wretched as Mary! Many of them wind up being dead."

True, but let's not get nitpicky. The point is, our health-care system is a terrible mess. It's expensive, wasteful, inefficient, unresponsive, and infested with lawyers. Which is why there has been a big push, in some quarters, to place it under the management of . . .

The federal government.

This is like saying that if your local police department has a corruption problem, the solution is to turn law enforcement over to the Sopranos. Nevertheless, there really are people— intelligent, educated, well-meaning people—who seriously believe that we should let Washington redesign our health-care system. It goes without saying that these people live and work in Washington; that's the only place where you're going to find intelligent, educated, well-meaning people who are that stupid.

The rest of the country is not so thrilled about trusting their health care to the same government that produced, for example, the U.S. Tax Code. Most Americans outside of Washington don't really trust Washington to do anything except screw up. This is the fundamental reason why we have a two-party political system. We put the Republicans in office until they have totally screwed things up, then we vote them out and let the Democrats take their turn totally screwing everything up, then we switch back to the Republicans, and so on, back and forth. It's like a Ping-Pong game in which neither player ever actually makes contact with the ball.

So to summarize the health-care crisis:

- Our current system for providing medical care is insane.
- But a majority of Americans understand that the federal government, if given the opportunity, would figure out a way to make it worse.
- Therefore, the odds are that nothing will be done.

So your best bet, until further notice, is to do what 83 percent of all licensed American physicians do, according to a recent survey: Avoid medical care altogether. This means you need to stay healthy. Exercise regularly, get plenty of rest, avoid contact with humans, and never inhale or open your eyes in a public restroom. Above all, make sure you eat a balanced diet. By which I mean: broccoli *and* alcohol.

Colonoscopy

~~~~~~~~

This is the only essay in this book that was originally published elsewhere; it ran in the Miami Herald, other newspapers, and on the Internet in 2008. I wanted to include it in this book because it's one of those rare instances when I wrote something with an actual point.

This essay produced quite a response; I'll tell you about it when you finish.

OK. You turned fifty. You know you're supposed to get a colonos-copy. But you haven't. Here are your reasons:

1. You've been busy.
2. You don't have a history of cancer in your family.
3. You haven't noticed any problems.
4. You don't want a doctor to stick a tube seventeen thousand feet up your butt.

Let's examine these reasons one at a time. No, wait, let's not. Because you and I both know that the only real reason is No. 4. This is natural. The idea of having another human, even a medical human, becoming deeply involved in what is techni-cally known as your "behindular zone" gives you the creeping willies.

I know this because I am like you, except worse. I yield to nobody in the field of being a pathetic weenie medical coward. I become faint and nauseous during even very minor medical procedures, such as making an appointment by phone. It's much worse when I come into physical contact with the medical profession. More than one doctor's office has a dent in the floor caused by my forehead striking it seconds after I got a shot.

In 1997, when I turned fifty, everybody told me I should get a colonoscopy. I agreed that I definitely should, but not right away. By following this policy, I reached age fifty-five without having had a colonoscopy. Then I did something so pathetic and embarrassing that I am frankly ashamed to tell you about it.

What happened was, a giant forty-foot replica of a human colon came to Miami Beach. Really. It's an educational exhibit called the Colossal Colon, and it was on a nationwide tour to promote awareness of colorectal cancer. The idea is, you crawl through the Colossal Colon, and you encounter various educational items in there, such as polyps, cancer, and hemorrhoids the size of regulation volleyballs, and you go, "Whoa, I better find out if I contain any of these things," and you get a colonoscopy.

If you are a professional humor writer, and there is a giant colon within a two-hundred-mile radius, you are legally obligated to go see it. So I went to Miami Beach and crawled through the Colossal Colon. I wrote a column about it, making tasteless colon jokes. But I also urged everyone to get a colonoscopy. I even, when I emerged from the Colossal Colon, signed a pledge stating that I would get one.

But I didn't get one. I was a fraud, a hypocrite, a liar. I was practically a member of Congress.

Five more years passed. I turned sixty, and I still hadn't gotten a colonoscopy. Then, a couple of weeks ago, I got an e-mail from my brother Sam, who is ten years younger than I am, but more mature. The e-mail was addressed to me and my middle brother, Phil. It said:

"Dear Brothers,

"I went in for a routine colonoscopy and got the dreaded diagnosis: cancer. We're told it's early and that there is a good prognosis that they can get it all out, so, fingers crossed, knock on wood, and all that. And of course they told me to tell my siblings to get screened. I imagine you both have."

Um. Well.

First I called Sam. He was hopeful, but scared. We talked for a while, and when we hung up, I called my friend Andy Sable, a gastroenterologist, to make an appointment for a colonoscopy. A few days later, in his office, Andy showed me a color diagram of the colon, a lengthy organ that appears to go all over the place, at one point passing briefly through Minneapolis. Then Andy explained the colonoscopy procedure to me in a thorough, reassuring, and patient manner. I nodded thoughtfully, but I didn't really hear anything he said, because my brain was shrieking, quote, "HE'S GOING TO STICK A TUBE SEVENTEEN THOUSAND FEET UP YOUR BUTT!"

I left Andy's office with some written instructions, and a prescription for a product called "MoviPrep," which comes in a box large enough to hold a microwave oven. I will discuss Movi-Prep in detail later; for now suffice it to say that we must never allow it to fall into the hands of America's enemies.

I spent the next several days productively sitting around being nervous. Then, on the day before my colonoscopy, I began my preparation. In accordance with my instructions, I didn't eat any solid food that day; all I had was chicken broth, which is basically water, only with less flavor. Then, in the evening, I took the MoviPrep. You mix two packets of powder together in a one-liter plastic jug, then you fill it with lukewarm water. (For those unfamiliar with the metric system, a liter is about 32 gallons.) Then you have to drink the whole jug. This takes about an hour, because MoviPrep tastes—and here I am being kind—like a mixture of goat spit and urinal cleanser, with just a hint of lemon.

The instructions for MoviPrep, clearly written by somebody with a great sense of humor, state that after you drink it, "a loose watery bowel movement may result." This is kind of like saying that after you jump off your roof, you may experience contact with the ground.

MoviPrep is a nuclear laxative. I don't want to be too graphic here, but: Have you ever seen a space shuttle launch? This is pretty much the MoviPrep experience, with you as the shuttle. There are times when you wish the commode had a seat belt. You spend several hours pretty much confined to the bathroom, spurting violently. You eliminate *everything*. And then, when you figure you must be totally empty, you have to drink *another* liter of MoviPrep, at which point, as far as I can tell, your bowels travel into the future and start eliminating food that you have not even *eaten* yet.

After an action-packed evening, I finally got to sleep. The next morning my wife drove me to the clinic. I was very nervous. Not only was I worried about the procedure, but I had been experiencing occasional return bouts of MoviPrep spurtage. I was thinking, "What if I spurt on Andy?" How do you apologize to a friend for something like that? Flowers would not be enough.

At the clinic I had to sign many forms acknowledging that I understood and totally agreed with whatever the hell the forms said. Then they led me to a room full of other colonoscopy people, where I went inside a little curtained space and took off my clothes and put on one of those hospital garments designed by sadist perverts, the kind that, when you put it on, makes you feel even more naked than when you are actually naked.

Then a nurse named Eddie put a little needle in a vein in my left hand. Ordinarily I would have fainted, but Eddie was very good, and I was already lying down. Eddie also told me that some people put vodka in their MoviPrep. At first I was ticked off that I hadn't thought of this, but then I pondered what would happen if you got yourself too tipsy to make it to the bathroom, so you were staggering around in full Fire Hose Mode. You would have no choice but to burn your house.

When everything was ready, Eddie wheeled me into the procedure room, where Andy was waiting with a nurse and an anesthesiologist. I did not see the seventeen-thousand-foot tube, but I knew Andy had it hidden around there somewhere. I was seriously nervous at this point. Andy had me roll over on my left side, and the anesthesiologist began hooking something up to the needle in my hand. There was music playing in the room, and I realized that the song was "Dancing Queen" by Abba. I remarked to Andy that, of all the songs that could be playing during this particular procedure, "Dancing Queen" has to be the least appropriate.

"You want me to turn it up?" said Andy, from somewhere behind me.

"Ha-ha," I said.

And then it was time, the moment I had been dreading for more than a decade. If you are squeamish, prepare yourself, because I am going to tell you, in explicit detail, exactly what it was like.

I have no idea. Really. I slept through it. One moment, Abba was shrieking *"Dancing Queen! Feel the beat from the tambourine . . ."*

. . . and the next moment, I was back in the other room, waking up in a very mellow mood. Andy was looking down at me and asking me how I felt. I felt excellent. I felt even more excellent when Andy told me that it was all over, and that my colon had passed with flying colors. I have never been prouder of an internal organ.

But my point is this: In addition to being a pathetic medical weenie, I was a complete moron. For more than a decade I avoided getting a procedure that was, essentially, nothing. There was no pain and, except for the MoviPrep, no discomfort. I was risking my life for nothing.

If my brother Sam had been as stupid as I was—if, when he turned fifty, he had ignored all the medical advice and avoided getting screened—he still would have had cancer. He just wouldn't have known. And by the time he did know—by the time he felt symptoms—his situation would have been much, much more serious. But because he was a grown-up, the doctors caught the cancer early, and they operated and took it out. Sam is now recovering and eating what he describes as "really, really boring food." His prognosis is good, and everybody is optimistic, fingers crossed, knock on wood, and all that.

Which brings us to you, Mr. or Mrs. or Miss or Ms. Over-Fifty-and-Hasn't-Had-a-Colonoscopy. Here's the deal: You either have colorectal cancer, or you don't. If you do, a colonoscopy will enable doctors to find it and do something about it. And if you don't have cancer, believe me, it's very reassuring to *know* you don't. There is no sane reason for you not to have it done.

I am so eager for you to do this that I am going to induce

you with an Exclusive Limited Time Offer. If you, after reading this, get a colonoscopy, let me know by sending a self-addressed, stamped envelope to Dave Barry Colonoscopy Inducement, *The Miami Herald*, 1 Herald Plaza, Miami, FL 33132. I will send you back a certificate, signed by me and suitable for framing if you don't mind framing a cheesy certificate, stating that you are a grown-up who got a colonoscopy. Accompanying this certificate will be a square of limited-edition custom-printed toilet paper with an image of Miss Paris Hilton on it. You may frame this also, or use it in whatever other way you deem fit.

But even if you don't want this inducement, please get a colonoscopy. If I can do it, you can do it. Don't put it off. Just do it.

Be sure to stress that you want the non-Abba version.

Postscript

This essay got a huge reaction—bigger than anything else I've ever written except the time I criticized Neil Diamond, which I will never do again. My colonoscopy story went viral on the Internet; many, many people wrote me to say it inspired them to get colonoscopies. Even now, more than a year later, people keep telling me about their colons. I'll get on an airplane, and somebody I don't know, sitting five rows away, will yell, "Dave! I had my colon checked! Everything looks good!"

"Great!" I'll say, starting to make a thumbs-up gesture, then

stopping when I realize that the other passengers might misinterpret it.

Anyway, it was a good thing for some of these people that they got screened, because their doctors found things that needed to be taken care of. Which is why you should get screened, too, if you're due. Or overdue. Just do it.

p.s. My brother Sam is doing fine.

A Practical, Workable Plan for Saving the Newspaper Business

I Sure Don't Have One

The American newspaper industry is in serious trouble.

How serious? Consider: In 1971, when I was hired for my first newspaper job, there were 62 million newspaper subscribers in the United States; today, according to the Audit Bureau of Circulation, there are twelve, an estimated five of whom are dead and therefore unlikely to renew.

What the heck happened?

I can hear you wiseacres answering: "You already told us what happened. They hired *you*."

Fair enough. Some of the blame is definitely mine. Over the years I've received at *least* 62 million letters from irate people declaring their intention to cancel their subscriptions because of something I wrote. Among the groups I have deeply offended are:

- Neil Diamond fans;
- People who don't think it's funny when you make untrue statements such as that George Washington invented the airplane;
- Cat owners;
- People who insist on being addressed as "doctor" because they have Ph.D.'s, as if these degrees represent an important achievement, rather than a reluctance to leave college;
- Appliance salespeople who try to sell you a service warranty for every damn thing you buy including batteries;
- People who react angrily to criticism of the *Lord of the Ring* movies, especially the suggestion that you were not totally awed by the walking, talking, kung-fu-fighting trees;[1]
- Barry Manilow fans;
- . . . and of course
- Lawyers.

This is a very incomplete list of the readers I managed to irritate. I once wrote a column that offended an entire *state*. Granted, it was North Dakota,[2] which has a smaller population than the average New York City public restroom. But still, those unhappy North Dakotans were newspaper readers, and therefore customers. And anybody who knows anything about business knows you should not offend your customers.

1. When I wrote that column, I received hate mail *written in Elvish*.
2. Yes! North Dakota is a state! Although it shares its capital (Montpelier) with Wyoming.

Of course that's part of the problem: The American newspaper industry isn't run by people who know anything about business. It's run mostly by English majors, or people who majored in some other academic sector of the gigantic bullshit festival known as "the liberal arts." We spent our college careers discussing and writing papers about large important books such as *Crime and Punishment* that often we were unable to physically read more than about 30 percent of because we were busy being college students. Our chief marketable skill, coming out of college, is the ability to write authoritatively about things we don't necessarily understand.

The newspaper business is a perfect fit for us, because it doesn't require the firm grasp on factual reality demanded by businesses such as, for example, plumbing. When a plumber installs a bathroom, he has to understand and obey the laws of plumbing physics, and he has to have all of the plumbing parts he needs, or the bathroom is not going to work, and he is not going to get paid. Whereas we journalists, using our English-major skills, are able to routinely assemble authoritative-sounding stories even though we have only a few tiny shreds of second- or third-hand information and only the vaguest understanding of what actually happened. We produce stories that, if they were bathrooms, would have water spurting from the electrical outlets and bolts of electricity shooting out of the toilet.

I produced many such stories myself, starting out as a cub reporter in West Chester, Pa., for a daily local newspaper called, descriptively, the *Daily Local News*. I wrote stories about a wide range of topics I was unqualified to discuss with any degree of authority, including municipal government, crime, fires, traffic accidents, the courts, the public schools, politics, medicine, zoning, religion, sewage treatment, and local residents who had grown unusually large zucchini. I always tried to be accurate, but I suspect I made mistakes of varying sizes in every story I wrote, including about the zucchini, which I probably identified as some other vegetable, or possibly a raccoon.

"Wait a minute," you're saying. "Don't newspapers have editors?"

Yes, but the editors are also English majors. What is worse, they are English majors who have ceased engaging directly in journalism. They spend virtually all of their time in conference-room story-planning meetings with other editors, and thus have completely lost touch with reality. Committees of newspaper editors are legendary for coming up with story ideas that would require reporters to perform feats of journalism that are clearly impossible, such as interview both Prince Charles *and* Jimmy Hoffa. Having dreamed up a story concept, the editors order some wretched reporter to execute it; when the reporter turns in the story, the editors are invariably disappointed that it doesn't measure up to the shining polished brilliance of the original idea as conceived in the conference room.

Editor meetings are also the source of almost all newspaper

"trend" stories, which over the years have consumed billions of acres of forestland without adding a single fact to the storehouse of human knowledge. These stories typically originate when an editor happens to notice something that strikes him or her as significant. For example, the editor might see a person wearing a Howdy Doody T-shirt, and then, a few hours later, see *another* person (or possibly even the same person; it doesn't matter) wearing a Howdy Doody T-shirt. The next day, at one of the story-planning meetings, the editor might mention this, and another editor might report having *also* recently seen a person (also possibly the same person) in a Howdy Doody T-shirt.

The editors, having reached critical mass—*Three* Howdy Doody T-shirts!—decide that they have discovered a trend. They stride out into the newsroom, where reporters, seeing them coming, scatter like gazelles on an African plain when the lions show up. Some reporters will dive under their desks to avoid being assigned a trend story.

Inevitably the editors track down some unfortunate reporter and order him to produce a thirty-inch "fun" story about the Howdy Doody nostalgia trend that is sweeping the nation. And make no mistake: The reporter *will* produce that story. He has to. The editors have already scheduled a publication date and commissioned a fun graphic-design element; they would be *very* unhappy with the reporter if he threw a monkey wrench into the production line of journalism by reporting that there actually was no such trend. So using his journalism skills, he will scrape together a story containing the Minimum Acceptable Trend Story Factoid Content, consisting of:

- A statistical sample of three regular people, representing the nation, who can be prodded into providing quotes affirming that, sure, they like Howdy Doody; and
- One authority willing to give an authoritative analysis of the Howdy Doody trend.

The three regular people can be anybody, including if necessary friends or relatives of the reporter. The authority is usually a college professor. There is no topic that you cannot find a college professor willing to produce an instant, authoritative quote about.

So the reporter grinds out thirty inches on the Howdy Doody craze and turns it in. The story gets a big display—bigger than most stories involving actual news—because (a) the editors thought of it; (b) it was on the schedule; (c) they had a graphic-design element for it; and (d) it's fun! Editors for other newspapers or TV news may see the story and order *their* reporters to investigate, thereby setting off a chain reaction of Howdy-Doody-craze stories all over the country. It's even possible that there might actually BE a nationwide Howdy Doody craze. Or, it could be that just one lone individual happened to be wearing a Howdy Doody T-shirt. Nobody in the newspaper business will ever know for sure, and nobody will care, because as soon as the story is printed it's time to move on to the next story concept, which originated when an editor decided, based on two people he talked to at a party, that there is a trend toward converting to Buddhism.

I'm not saying that newspapers publish only stories about imaginary developments. They also publish box scores; horoscopes; Garfield; stock tables; movie listings; classified ads; deeply ponderous editorials in which an anonymous committee of editors in, say, Cleveland reveal what they think about, say, North Korea; Sudoku; letters from insane people; typographical errors; and the word jumble. Sometimes, when reporters are able to elude editorial supervision, they even publish actual news.

This has been the basic newspaper recipe for many decades, and until fairly recently it was hugely successful. Newspapers were raking in money, and they spent it freely. It was a golden age for us English majors. I was on the staff of the *Miami Herald*'s Sunday magazine, *Tropic*, and among the items I put on expense reports, and got reimbursed for, were:

- a four-day rental of a monkey costume;
- a three-day rental of a massive recreational vehicle that I used for the sole purpose of camping out overnight in the parking lot of a Wal-Mart located 27.8 miles from my house;
- a night at a strip club;

- a man-sized fiberglass goose; and
- many hundreds of alcoholic beverages, including one $50 drink at Nick G. Castrogiovanni's Original Big Train Bar in New Orleans called "A Wild Night at the Capri Motel," which was served in a large foam container shaped like a commode.

We journalists were fearless spenders of our newspapers' travel budgets in those days. In 1987, *The New York Times Magazine* discovered, about ten years late, that Miami had a drug and crime problem, and ran a big honking spectacularly clueless cover story called *Can Miami Save Itself?* In response, *Tropic* sent an investigative team consisting of me and photographer Chuck Fadely to New York City to conduct an intensive two-day probe to see if we could uncover any problems up there.[3] As part of our investigation we decided to have a look at the Islip, Long Island, garbage barge, which was this disgusting barge with a huge reeking pile of garbage on it that had become a big story because New York couldn't figure out how to get rid of it. At the time it was probably one of the two or three most famous barges in the world; it had become, in its own way, a celebrity, comparable to Lindsay Lohan.

By running up a ridiculous taxi bill, Chuck and I were able to locate the garbage barge somewhere off the coast of Brooklyn;

---

3. It turned out there were several.

however, Chuck couldn't get a really good picture of it. So we decided to rent a helicopter. Yes. We took a taxi to New Jersey and rented a chopper so we could fly over the harbor and *take a picture of garbage*. I don't remember exactly what it cost, but it was thousands of dollars, and the *Miami Herald* paid for it without batting an eye.

Another example: One time the editors of *Tropic*, Gene Weingarten and Tom Shroder, decided to do a cover story in which they offered a $200 prize for the reader who came up with the best idea for a new fad. The winner was a guy whose fad idea was eating money; he said that if he won, he would eat the prize, in cash. Which he did. In other words, the Sunday magazine of a major newspaper aided and abetted a person who *ate legal U.S. currency*. (Gene recalls: "I think we also donated two hundred dollars to charity. As if that made it any better.")

And it wasn't just the *Miami Herald* that was tossing money around. Many big newspapers had large travel budgets and far-flung bureaus staffed by reporters on generous expense accounts. The papers could afford it; they were making big profits. We journalists assumed that this was a result of the unquenchable public thirst for the vital journalism we were cranking out.

And then, *pffft*, it all went away. Today newspapers everywhere, if they're not shutting down completely, are laying people off and cutting expenses to the bone. Newspapers that used to send reporters all over the world now won't authorize any trip that would involve leaving the parking lot.

What the heck happened?

Again I hear the wiseacres: "What happened was, you rented a monkey suit *and* a helicopter."

True, but that's not the whole story. Another big factor was the Internet, which is an important trend that the newspaper industry discovered in approximately 1998. The Internet posed an unprecedented challenge to our business. We had long thought of ourselves as the ultimate collectors and distributors of timely information; suddenly we were being confronted with competition in the form of the most revolutionary, powerful, complex, fluid, cost-effective, and far-reaching information-technology development in human history. Fortunately, to meet this challenge, the newspaper industry had . . .

English majors!

They swung boldly into action, forming teams, holding many, many brainstorming meetings in conference rooms, and coming up with a variety of strategies for dealing with the Internet challenge. In the early going, the main two newspaper strategies were:

- Pretending there was no Internet.
- Redesigning newspapers so they *looked* like the Internet, but a special kind of Internet where the information was outdated and static, and you couldn't click on anything.

Unfortunately, neither of these strategies succeeded in defeating the Internet challenge. So newspapers switched, reluctantly, to a strategy of actually putting their stories on the Internet. At first the plan was to charge money for this content, but the public was not willing to pay for it. It turns out that the public is nowhere near as convinced of the value of journalism as journalists are.

So newspapers came up with a bold new plan: *not* charging money for their Internet content. This is the strategy we employ today, and it has been highly successful from a purely marketing standpoint. The public is very receptive to the idea of being able to read newspaper stories without paying for them. In fact, many people have canceled their subscriptions and read newspaper content exclusively online. This makes sense, from a consumer standpoint: If you went to a gas station, and they offered you two pricing plans—Plan A, in which you paid for your gas, or Plan B, in which you got exactly the same gas for free—you would have to have the economic IQ of a rutabaga[4] to choose Plan A.

So the good news is that, thanks to our current strategy, lots of people are reading newspaper stories. We know this because we can measure "hits," which indicate how many people have looked at a story online. Newspaper people these days get very excited about "hits." Unfortunately, all these "hits" produce very little "money." So newspapers have been laying off people, including many of the reporters who produce the actual stories. At the same time, newspaper editors are ordering the dwindling number

4. Or the United States Congress.

of reporters to spend more and more of their time engaging in non-journalism, non-revenue-producing Internet activities such as Facebooking, making videos, podcasting, blogging, tweeting, fwirping,[5] etc. The strategic thinking here is: "Hey, *other* people are doing these things on the Internet, so we should, too! We might get 'hits'!"

So to sum up the situation: Newspapers are not making money on the Internet, and have decided that the solution is to do more things on the Internet that do not make money. Everybody hopes that somehow—nobody can say how—this will enable newspapers to survive. It's like the classic 1998 episode of *South Park* in which the boys discover that gnomes are sneaking into people's homes and stealing their underpants. The boys visit the gnomes' secret underground lair and find a huge mound of underpants. The boys ask why, and the gnomes explain that they have a three-phase business plan, which is:

Phase 1—Collect underpants
Phase 2—?
Phase 3—Profit

This is basically the current newspaper plan, except with the Internet instead of underpants. We have NO idea what's sup-

5. There actually is no such thing as fwirping, but if there were, and it was something that people were doing on the Internet, editors would order reporters to do it.

posed to happen in Phase 2. But if things keep going the way they are, in a few years the newspaper industry will be down to one reporter, who will sit in the middle of the newsroom watching cable-TV news and frantically cranking out 140-character news tweets under the supervision of two or three dozen editors.

That's the bleak future of newspaper journalism unless somebody can come up with a plan to save it. Fortunately, I have such a plan. Unfortunately, it involves using time travel to go back to 1971.

So we're doomed. Within the next decade or so, newspaper journalism, as we know it, is essentially going to disappear. *Then* the public will be sorry! Unless there's something else to read on the Internet or watch on TV, in which case the public won't care.

Either way, it's over.

This makes me sad. For one thing, it was a *lot* of fun. For another thing, the newspaper business, despite its many flaws, managed to do a lot of good. And it employed, in its newsrooms, the smartest, hardest-working, funniest, quirkiest, most cynical and at the same time idealistic group of borderline insane people I've ever known. As newspapers fade away, I raise my glass in a farewell toast to all those wonderful colleagues, and in memory of the glory years.

Speaking of which, my glass is actually a foam commode.

Judaism for
Christians

My wife is Jewish, and I am not. Most of the time this is not a problem, because neither of us is what I would call strongly religious. Especially not me. If I had a religion, it would be called jokeatarianism. We jokeatarians believe it's *possible* that an all-powerful, all-knowing God created the Earth and all its creatures, but if He did, He was obviously kidding.

I was, however, raised in a Christian household, and sometimes I feel the influence of my upbringing. This happens mainly at Christmas, when I engage in traditional rituals such as making a series of frantic, nearly random retail purchases; overeating; buying a Christmas tree; complaining about how much the Christmas tree costs; getting sap in my hair while wrestling with the tree in a futile effort to make it stand up straight even though it has some kind of tree scoliosis; and spending the better part of an evening untangling the five-thousand-bulb string of lights that has, using its natural defense mechanism, wadded itself into a dense snarl the size of a croquet ball.

Also at Christmas I like to engage in "wassailing." This sounds like a kind of violent assault ("Fred wassailed Herb upside his head") but is actually an old English word meaning to drink a festive beverage and sing traditional Christmas carols such as "We Wish You a Merry Christmas," verse two of which goes:

Oh bring us a figgy pudding
Oh bring us a figgy pudding
Oh bring us a figgy pudding
And bring it right here!

This carol dates back to seventeenth-century England, when groups of carolers would go from house to house demanding figgy puddings. If they didn't get one, they would break down the front door (using a fruitcake), then barge inside and wassail on the occupants. This was the origin of both Halloween and soccer.

But aside from that, I am not devout; I almost never attend church unless somebody I know is getting married or has expired. My wife, on the other hand, does go to services at the synagogue. But here's one big difference between Christians and Jews: Whereas Christians break their worship time down into manageable chunks by attending services every Sunday through-out the year, many Jews, my wife among them, do *not* go to synagogue for most of the year, then compensate for this by worshipping for as many as fourteen thousand straight hours *in a single day.*

You may think this is impossible, but that's because you are not, as far as I know, married to my wife. I am, and here's what happens. Every few months she'll say to me, out of the blue, "You remember that tomorrow is Harish Kadoma, right?"

(She doesn't actually say "Harish Kadoma." I'm just using that as an example of what it *sounds* like she's saying.)

And I'll say, "Is it important? Because I have plans tomorrow." (These plans typically involve watching old episodes of *Reno 911* on TiVo, but I do not say this.)

And she'll get this exasperated look and say, "I told you to put it on your calendar. It's the second most holy day in the Jewish year."

(Sometimes she says it's the third. As far as I can tell, every Jewish holy day ranks, holiness-wise, either second or third.)

When this happens, my heart sinks, because I know this means she's going to go to services at the synagogue, which means *I'm* going to services at the synagogue. My wife always says: "If you really don't want to go, you don't have to." But as you veteran married men know, this is Wife Code for: "If you really don't want to go, you still have to."

So the next day I put on my least comfortable suit and we drive to the synagogue. Actually we can't drive all the way, because on Jewish holy days everybody goes to the synagogue, so we have to park in an adjacent state and walk from there. Usually when we arrive the service has been going on for several hours, which means it's just getting started.

I've found that in many ways the Jewish worship service is similar to a Christian service. You sit down; you stand up; you sit back down; you remark frequently, as a group, on how great God is; you check your watch and note that it is 10:31 A.M. and vow not to keep checking because it only makes time go slower; you wonder if you could get away with very subtly checking your text messages and decide it is probably not worth incurring the wrath of God or, worse, your wife; you stand back up; you sit back down; you try to remember the name of the movie starring Kevin Bacon that has essentially the same plot as *Jaws* except it's set in the Nevada desert and instead of a giant man-eating shark it has giant man-eating worms capable of underground speeds approaching fifty miles per hour; you stand back up; you finally think of a really clever comeback you could have used on the guy who was being a jerk at your daughter's basketball game several months earlier; you sit back down; you mentally recite the lyrics to "Maybelline," Chuck Berry's masterpiece song about two fast cars and one unfaithful woman, including the greatest couplet ever written about automotive thermodynamics, *"Rainwater*

blowin' all under my hood / I knew that was doin' my motor good";
you speculate on what the giant worms had supposedly been
surviving on out there in the desert before they started eating
movie actors; you stand back up; you sit back down; your leg
falls asleep; *you* fall asleep; your wife elbows you awake because you are making a noise like a warthog with a nasal infec-
tion; you remember, with a feeling of triumph, that the Kevin
Bacon movie was called *Tremors*; you decide to reward yourself
by sneaking another peek at your watch; your mood turns to
despair when you see that the time is *still* 10:31 A.M. And so on.

Some Jewish holy day services are highlighted by a dramatic
moment when a man gets up in front of everybody and blows on
a "shofar," which is the horn of a ram. As you can imagine, this
really upsets the ram.

I'm kidding; the horn is no longer attached to the ram. The
ram (and I envy it) is elsewhere, possibly watching old episodes
of *Reno 911* on TiVo. But the blowing of the shofar is still considered a highlight because it means you have reached the cli-
max of the service, which means there's only about fourteen
more hours to go.

After the service there is usually eating. Or sometimes there
is fasting. Either way, there is a lot of thinking about food. Food
is extremely important in the Jewish religion; the word "brisket"
alone appears more than 950 times in the Torah. The food con-
nection is especially strong on Passover, the second or third most

holy holiday in the Jewish calendar, which commemorates the Exodus, when the Israelites escaped from Egypt, pursued by giant man-eating worms.

No, seriously, they were pursued by the Egyptians, and on Passover Jewish people hold a special meal called a seder, in which a lot of the food is symbolic. For example, when the Israelites were fleeing Egypt, they did not have time to let their bread rise, so at the seder you are served matzo, which is a very sturdy construction-grade unleavened cracker measuring about eighteen square feet, which you can either eat, sleep under, or break a sharp piece off of for use as a weapon against the Egyptians. Also you drink wine, which symbolizes the fact that, hey, there's wine.

My favorite part of the seder is the reciting of the 10 Plagues of Egypt, which God used to convince Pharaoh to free the Israelites. This story illustrates one major difference between me and God. If I were an all-powerful supreme being, I would appear before Pharaoh and order him to let the Israelites go, and if he said no, FWOOM,[1] there would be a lightning bolt, and when the smoke cleared, there would be a Pharaoh-shaped smear on the floor. Then I would look around the room in a casual yet menacing manner and ask to speak with the Vice Pharaoh. In other words, I would be an unsubtle, straight-ahead, Dick Cheney style of supreme being.

God was much cooler. He sent Moses to speak to the Pharaoh,

1. That's right: If I were God, lightning would go FWOOM.

and when the Pharaoh refused to free the Israelites, inflicted an escalating series of plagues on Egypt, including flies, cattle disease, lice, hail, boils, locusts, and fruitcake.

No, I'm kidding about the fruitcake. God wasn't *that* wrathful. But He did send the other plagues, and I always look forward to reciting them during the seder because one of them is: frogs. Yes! God caused Egypt to be *overrun with frogs*. That kind of originality is exactly why we call Him the supreme being. And if you don't think frogs sounds like a scary plague, you don't know my mother-in-law. She is *terrified* of frogs. Once, when we were supposed to have dinner with her, she called to tell us that she couldn't leave her condominium building because there was a frog outside the door. Seriously. We tried to convince her that there was no real danger, but she wouldn't listen. In her mind, the frog was waiting out there *specifically for her*. If she went outside, her lifeless body would be found the next morning in the bushes, covered with what the coroner would later identify as several thousand tongue marks, and *then* we would be sorry.

I realize that if you were raised, as I was, in a Christian household, some of these Jewish traditions may seem strange, even weird (although I have yet to encounter anything in the Jewish tradition any weirder than, say, the Easter Bunny). But I believe, based on my experience attending both Christian and Jewish worship services, that the two religions have a lot in common. To help you see what I mean, I've created the following chart comparing Judaism and Christianity:

Religious Issues	Judaism	Christianity
God: Great? Or What?	Great	Great
Sin: OK? Or Not?	Not	Not
Frogs?	Yes	No
Figgy Pudding?	No	Yes

Yes, there are differences. But in my view they are not as significant as the similarities. I believe that if we could all focus less on what divides us, and more on what we agree on, this would be a better and happier world, both here and in the hereafter, for people of all religions. Except of course for us jokeatarians. We're definitely going to wind up in hell. Surrounded by fruitcake.

Fangs of Endearment

~~~~~~~~~~~~~~~~

A Vampire Novel

Warning

With a feeling of ominous foreboding based on the cliff-hanger ending of the last book, I turned my battered old pickup truck into the last remaining parking spot outside Creepstone High School. I glanced in the rearview mirror and scrunched my forehead in dismay as I realized for the millionth time that I do not consider myself at all attractive, although roughly 85 percent of the male characters I encounter either fall in love with me or want to kill me, or both, and in the movie version I am portrayed by a total babe.

Heaving a sigh of exasperation, I creaked open the truck door and, with my trademark charming clumsiness, fell out face-first. But before I hit the asphalt, Phil was there to catch me, having covered the seventy-five yards from his luxury car to my truck in two-tenths of a second, although fortunately nobody noticed this because Phil is brilliantly clever, and the other students at Creepstone High have the observational skills of boiled ham.

Phil swooped me into his arms using the super vampire strength that he has in addition to his super vampire speed and his ability to read minds, perform complex mathematical calculations in his head, assemble a working nuclear submarine entirely from clock parts, and recite all the lyrics to *Guys and Dolls* backward.

"Good morning," he breathed calmly.

For a moment I was unable to respond, because I was so stunned, as I will be many, many more times in this novel, by how unbelievably handsome he is, with his perfect face and chiseled cheekbones, and his gorgeous eyes that change color depending on how recently he has sucked all the blood out of a live bear, and his perfectly teased hair tousling down over his broad gorgeous forehead speckled with beautiful little perfect beads of condensation caused by the fact that he has the same body temperature as an Eskimo Pie. Even through my unfashionable dress that I was wearing because I don't care about fashion despite being so attractive to men, I could feel the chill of his granite-hard arms. It was like being hefted by a robot that had spent the night in a cold meat locker. I was in heaven.

"Put me down," I insisted in a tone of determined insistence.

"Why?" he questioned, arching a single perfect gorgeous eyebrow into a quizzical arch.

"I have to get to class," I asserted, struggling ineffectively to escape his powerful yet sensitive grasp.

"There's plenty of time," he retorted, with a twisting smirk of his perfect lips.

"Maybe for *you*," I objected with a wry smile.

We can engage in this kind of witty banter for pages on end.

Finally relenting with a sigh, Phil gently set me down on the parking lot and took my hand in his strong and perfect hand that he sometimes lovingly immerses in my Coke Zero to cool it to exactly the right temperature. Walking toward the school, we were joined by Phil's brothers and sisters, who are all also gorgeous brilliant wealthy sophisticated centuries-old vampires posing as high-school students for reasons that are never totally clear.

As we entered the school I felt Phil's grip tighten, possibly fracturing my ring and index fingers. Looking up I saw the reason: Stewart was striding toward us in an ominous way. Stewart is a member of an indigenous tribe of Native

Americans who become werewolves at puberty, in addition to developing acne. They do not get along with the vampires. One time in boys' phys. ed. the two sides played each other in volleyball, and before it was over seven civilian students had been disemboweled. This could have created a real stink had not the Creepstone High authorities, who are even less observant than the student body, concluded that the cause was an unusually fast-acting stomach flu.

But tensions still simmered, as I could see by the dark look in Stewart's brooding, smoldering, husky eyes. He is not as handsome as Phil, who makes Brad Pitt look like a yak butt. But he is still attractive in his own lanky darkly smoldering indigenous tribal way, and it goes without saying that he is in love with me and wants to marry me. I'm in love with him, too, but not as much as I am with Phil, who if all goes well is going to make me a vampire soon so we can spend all eternity being gorgeous and sensitive and sucking on bears together. I long for that day, but I hate knowing that I am hurting Stewart so badly by being so attractive to him without trying to or consciously realizing that I am.

Hello, Stewart, I mouthed with a facial expression of sorrowful chagrin.

He looked at Phil with a look of pure lanky indigenous hatred before turning to me and replying, with a voice drenched in the aching and smoldering longingness of a powerful emotion that I knew he could never express in words, "Hello."

"What do you want?" hissed Phil with anger through his perfect white teeth, although not the ones that were currently retracted.

"I'm not talking to you, leech," retorted Stewart with a flash of anger that made me worry that he was about to sprout full-body fur and teeth the size of steak knives, which could lead to bloodshed, death, and—if the school authorities witnessed it—detention.

"*Stop* it, you two," I protested, my heart filling with despair at how much these two attractive males, despite being mortal enemies with completely different lifestyles and diets, were so much alike in the sense of being insanely crazy for me. "What is it, Stewart?" I added in a sincere voice of concerned friendship.

He looked at me with his dark lanky eyes, and for a moment I saw in his expression the thoughtful and caring young man with whom I had shared so many emotional moments in the previous book without ever actually doing it. Suddenly his expression changed to one of dark foreboding. "If you go out in the woods today," he whispered hoarsely, "you better not go alone."

"What . . ." I protested elliptically. But Stewart was already striding lankily away. I turned to Phil, but before I could speak I was struck dumb by the perfection of his chiseled cheekbones, and the realization that, of all the girls in the world, I was the one he found irresistibly attractive, as so many males do, although for the life of me I don't see why because as far as I am concerned there is nothing special about me, me, me. Phil was watching Stewart's back, and on his impossibly handsome face I could see an expression of anger mixed with worry, and possibly thirst.

Finally finding my voice, I inquired, "What did he mean by that?"

"Mean by what?" replied Phil flatly.

"About me not going into the woods alone," I clarified.

Phil turned his perfect gaze upon me, causing me to be once again struck by how gorgeous etc. etc. "I'm sure it's nothing," he soothed calmly, adding, "I'm especially sure it's not Denise the vengeful psychopathic female vampire from the previous book who has vowed to hunt you down and torture you to death and who has been sighted recently in the woods around Creepstone. There is definitely no need to worry about *that*," he added with a quick glance at his brothers and sisters, who sprinted off toward the woods at speeds in excess of 180 miles per hour.

Despite Phil's reassurance, there was something in his tone that troubled me. But what was it? What had Stewart been trying to tell me? Was something bad about to happen? Would I soon find myself in yet another dramatic plot situation filled with peril? And why *did* everybody find me so attractive?

Before I could answer these questions, the bell rang.

"I have to get to calculus class!" I exclaimed with rue, adding, "There's a test today."

"You'll do fine," kidded Phil with an impish grin on his perfect features.

"Not if I don't get there!" I bantered in reply as I turned with such haste that in my endearing clumsiness I would have smashed face-first into the large plate-glass main door if Phil had not yanked it off its hinges with one hand and flung it aside, decapitating two freshmen. They were not major characters, but I could not help but wonder, as I hurried off to class, if this was an omen of bad things to come.

CHAPTER TWO

Decision

"How was school today?" inquired my father, Pete, looking up from the newspaper as he sat at the kitchen table in our modest home where we live together without my mother, who divorced my father and lives with her new husband in Florida and appears only sporadically as needed.

"Fine," I responded noncommittally as I removed a Swanson's Hungry Man Chicken Burrito dinner from the oven and set it down.

"Ouch," he retorted, because with my endearing clumsiness I had set it on his forearm.

"Sorry!" I exclaimed in dismay.

"Don't worry," he sighed with his usual stoic calm as a blister the size of a hockey puck appeared on his skin next to the eight-inch scar from the time I made shish kebabs. "Listen," he continued, "you seem a little distracted lately. Is there something wrong?"

I hesitated. Pete is chief of police of Creepstone, but he is not exactly Sherlock Holmes, if you catch my drift. He has so far failed to pick up on the fact that my boyfriend is a vampire who spends every night in my room, and that my other boyfriend is a werewolf, and that Creepstone, not to mention the entire state of Washington, is teeming with violent homicidal supernatural creatures, about 60 percent of whom are trying to kill me personally.

"No," I responded simply. "There's nothing wrong."

Satisfied, Pete grunted and returned to his paper. Then, remembering something in his mind, he looked up again.

"By the way," he intoned, "I want you to stay out of the woods."

I gasped and dropped my fork, which penetrated about a half-inch into Pete's foot.

"Why?" I inquired forebodingly.

"There's been some trouble," he expressed with a wince as he pulled the fork out and put it on the table out of my reach.

"What kind of trouble?" I probed.

"In the past two days, a hundred and fifty-eight hikers have been killed in the woods around Creepstone."

"Killed?" I queried. I felt a cold feeling shoot through my veins like an intravenous Slushie. "How?" I elaborated.

"It's the darnedest thing," marveled Pete. "All of them were violently dismembered, apparently by someone or something with incredibly savage strength. Some of the victims' limbs were found as far as two football fields away from their bodies."

I stared at him with a facial expression of shock.

"But how . . ." I began, searching for the words to complete the question that was even then forming in my brain. "How did *two football fields* get into the woods?"

Pete shook his head and shrugged, raising and lowering his shoulders to indicate he didn't know the answer. "That's got us stumped so far," he expressed ruefully. "Also we can't figure out what's killing all these hikers. I mean, sure, we usually get two or three violent-dismemberment hiker deaths a week around here; that's been going on as long as anybody can remember. But a hundred and fifty-eight dead in two days seems like a lot. Doc Smelkins examined all of the body pieces we were able to find, and he ruled out natural causes such as hookworm."

"Then what could it be?" I persisted.

"Right now we're working on the theory that it could be a bobcat, or a pack of unusually aggressive squirrels. But until we get this thing figured out, I don't want you going out in the woods, OK?"

I nodded pensively, thinking. First Stewart had warned me not to go into the woods. Then Phil had also mentioned something about the woods . . . What was it?

At the thought of Phil, I allowed myself a small smile of happiness due to the fact that he is so incredibly beautiful and perfectly chiseled, and yet he still chose *me*—Me! With all my trademark quirks!—over all the other women in the world including Angelina Jolie. But then my forehead puckered into a frown as I remembered that Phil had mentioned that Denise the psychopathic vampire who was stalking me from the previous book had been sighted recently in the woods. Could she have something to do with the 158 slain hikers? Should I mention any of this to Pete? With all these people being slaughtered, and with him being responsible for the safety of the community, shouldn't I tell him about the imminent danger so he could protect himself and all the other innocent human lives being threatened?

Nah. The more I thought about it, the more I knew what I had to do: *I had to go out into the woods alone.* It seemed crazy, like the plot of a bad horror movie where the teenage girl hears a scary noise in the basement, but instead of doing what anybody with an IQ higher than a Chicken McNugget would do, namely sprint out of the house, she goes down into the basement. But I knew I had to do it, because that's what I always do with my trademark stubbornness: I place myself in grave plot peril when there is no coherent reason to do so. Some people may call this ridiculous, but I am guessing that "some people" have not sold 50 million books to date.

"I'm tired," I informed Pete, yawning with my mouth for emphasis. "I think I'll go up to my room now." I leaned over to give Pete a goodnight kiss, only to trip forward with my trademark heartwarming clumsiness and head-butt him in the temple. He went down like a sack of gravel, out cold on the kitchen floor, eyes open, pupils dilated. I decided it was best to leave him there. I knew that he couldn't do anything anyway. It was up to me. Only me. Me me me me me.

Just then the doorbell rang, interrupting my thought process. I wondered who it could be and decided to find out by opening the door. Doing so, I saw Sven Lindstrom, a tall, blond extremely handsome boy who's captain of the Creepstone High football team and incredibly popular. He could have any girl he wanted.

Oh no, I thought internally, knowing what was coming.

"I love you," he emoted.

"Sven," I spluttered, "I can't—"

"I know," he interrupted. "You already have Phil and Stewart. But I don't care. I love you, and although I could have any girl I want, I will always love only you. If it makes a difference, in addition to being extremely attractive physically, I am a member of the supernatural-American community."

"*You?*" I expostulated. "I thought you were of Swedish descent!"

"I am," he concurred. "But the males in my family carry a terrible curse. When we're under great emotional stress, we turn into . . ." Unable to complete the sentence, he looked downward toward the ground.

"Turn into what?" I pressed.

He raised his head and his piercing blue eyes bored into mine, although not literally.

"Zamboni machines," he blurted.

"No," I reacted in horror.

"Yes," he whispered hoarsely. "We transform, then break into skating rinks and resurface them repeatedly, whether they need it or not. We can't stop ourselves."

"I thought that was just a myth," I intoned wonderingly.

"I wish," he regretted.

I was afraid to ask the next question, but I could not stop myself, because of my trademark inability to cease emitting dialogue.

"What if there's no ice rink around?" I interrogated.

Tears streamed from his handsome Nordic eyes as a look of shame crept across his chiseled face like a fast-moving caterpillar of emotion.

"We'll do frozen ponds, or even driveways," he sobbed ashamedly. "Any reasonably level ice-covered surface." He put his head in his hands, sobbing. He had really nice hair.

"Sven," I commiserated, touching his shoulder with my hand. He was muscular, like Phil and Stewart. One thing about these attractive male supernatural beings: In addition to being crazy about me, they are in excellent physical condition. "It's not your fault," I added. "You can't help being what you are," I added further.

Feeling the touch of my hand touching him, Sven raised his head and looked at me with an expression that I had seen before in the past.

Not again, I reflected mentally.

"Marry me," he urged.

"Sven," I sighed. "I can't. I—"

"I will make you happy," he broke in persistently. "I will love you and worship you forever. And as God is my witness, you will never again have to contend with bumpy or pitted ice."

It was very tempting. But I knew, from previous experience with supernatural hunks who found me irresistible, that if I led Sven on—if I gave him even the slightest reason to hope that he could have me—I would only break his heart and probably place him in mortal danger of being killed. I knew I had to make it completely, undeniably clear to him that he had absolutely no chance, or his life would be ruined, and it would be all my fault.

"Maybe," I declared.

"Really?" he exclaimed, his eyes lighting up with joy like twin blue spherical orbs equipped with some kind of internal illumination.

"Yes," I allowed. Then, with my trademark unbelievably annoying emotional incoherence, I added: "No."

A look of confusion settled on Sven's perfectly chiseled Slavic cheekbones, unless I'm thinking of Nordic. I'm pretty sure it's one of those.

"Wait a minute," he puzzled. "I'm not sure whether you're saying yes, or no, or maybe."

"I am," I affirmed.

"You are *what?*" he pressed.

"Yes," I clarified.

"What?" he chagrinned.

Before I could answer, I felt a jolt as I suddenly remembered something: *the main story line*. Somehow, I had to get back to it.

"I'm sorry, Sven," I apologized. "I'm about to get myself in grave plot peril so I have to go."

"But . . ." he commenced.

"Maybe next book," I curtailed, closing the door in his perfectly chiseled Slavic (or Nordic) (I should look this up if I get time before this is published) features.

Through the door I heard a wail, followed by groans of pain, followed by clanking, followed by a motor starting, followed by the whooshing sound of sidewalk ice being re-surfaced in an emotional manner.

But I had no time to think about Sven. Right now I had to think about how anguished I was, with all these powerful feelings swirling around inside me like a smoothie being blended from a variety of emotional fruits as I stepped over Pete's body, nearly losing my footing in his drool puddle as I prepared to go out into the woods with nothing to protect me except my various attractive supernatural boyfriends. I did not know what peril I was about to face. All I knew was one thing, the most important thing of all:

Whatever happened, it would involve me.

CHAPTER THREE

Peril

I stumbled through the woods, tripping with clumsy en-dearingness over the logs that lay everywhere, like the corpses of dead trees knocked down by gravity. It was get-ting dark, and I knew that Phil would be out looking for me with his tawny eyes nestled in the chiseled perfection of his face. Stewart would also be looking for me in his lanky way with his bulging, rippling muscles or giant snout, depending on what form he was in. I knew that if Phil and Stewart ran into each other, they would probably get into a supernatural high-speed fight, and one or both of them could be badly injured or even killed, and it would be my fault because they were both so crazy mad in love with me.

I felt guilt gnawing at the pit of my stomach from within like a family of angry gastrointestinal ferrets. I wished I could die. I wished that a big electrical thing of lightning would come shooting down from the sky and kill me, or at least that an editor would cut out some of these interminable monologues about my feelings.

But I knew that could never happen, as it would be a violation of my contract. And so I continued to stumble endearingly forward as total darkness fell over the woods while a full moon rose into the sky to provide visibility for the climactic action sequence.

I came to a clearing completely surrounded on all sides by the dark forbidding woods. I walked into the clearing as the cold wind blew my hair around into a big trademark mess, although fortunately I don't care about hair or makeup because the last thing I need to do is make myself even *more* irresistible. With a feeling of even greater foreboding than usual, I kept walking forward, putting one leg in front of the other in an alternating sequence.

Suddenly, I saw movement at the far edge of the clearing. I stopped and stared. A chill slithered up my spine like an ascending iguana wearing tiny booties made from pieces of Fudgsicle as I saw the terrifying shadowy figure step menacingly into the clearing. With a shock of recognition I recognized who it was:

Barbara Walters.

No, sorry, there I go with my trademark endearing nearsightedness. As the shadowy figure drew nearer, I realized with a second shock of recognition that although she wore her hair the way Barbara Walters does, it was actually somebody far more dangerous; somebody who had been subtly foreshadowed in previous chapters:

Denise.

"So," she hissed, gliding vengefully forward as if on gliders.

I took a step back and stumbled over something. I screamed in horror as I realized that it was a human thigh—part of what had only days ago been a living, breathing hiker who, if he had been a male and cute and had met me, would probably have wanted to marry me. But now that was never to be, I reflected sorrowfully as I fell backward and landed on my back. I looked up to see Denise standing over me, her vampire eyes glowing with redness like two hot eyeball-sized coals.

"Please," I pleaded.

"So," she hissed again, and in that instant I realized that she was not big on dialogue. She bared her teeth, revealing her needle-like fangs, which glinted brightly in the moonlight like some kind of sharp highly reflective things used in a simile. I squinched my eyes shut, preparing myself to be killed in a horrible manner, which I knew I deserved after causing so much pain because of my uncontrollable irresistibility. The dramatic tension mounted to a fever pitch as I waited to feel Denise's teeth plunge vengefully into my neck and suck my blood out like a giant supernatural mosquito. I wondered how much it would hurt, and how long it would last before I was dead, and who, if anybody, would take over as narrator.

And just then it happened, a dramatic turn of events so unexpected and shocking that nobody could have predicted it in a million years without having read the previous books. I heard a snarling sound and opened my eyes to see that Denise, instead of attacking me, was fighting for her life. And the person she was fighting against—the person who, against all odds, had appeared at the last possible instant to rescue me, was:

Barbara Walters.

No, I am leavening the narrative with humor. It was really Phil. In the moonlight he looked more perfect and tawny-eyed and chiseled and gorgeous than ever. I still could not believe, as I watched him bite off Denise's right ear and, with characteristic godlike gracefulness, spit it into the woods, that he found me—Me! (Me!)—so attractive. I sighed, anticipating the moment when he was finished disassembling Denise so I could finally kiss his perfectly sculpted lips, despite the risk of frostbite.

But my fantasy was interrupted when his eyes flashed me an alarmed look of tawny ominousness.

"Run away!" he commanded.

"Why?" I questioned.

"They're coming!" he explained.

"Who's coming?" I prompted.

"They are," he elaborated as he pointed toward the edge of the clearing with Denise's left arm.

I looked in that direction, and my mouth gaped open as I saw them emerging from the woods:

The Gambinis.

They were a family of ancient and powerful vampires whom I had encountered in the previous book. They controlled all of the vampire activity in the world, as well as a large sector of the waste-management industry. It goes without saying that they were all really good-looking and obsessed with me.

"What do they want?" I inquired.

Phil scratched his tousled hair with Denise's hand. "Apparently they want to be part of the climactic action sequence," he postulated, adding, "and it appears there's going to be a lot of action." Using Denise's head, he nodded toward the opposite side of the clearing. My jaw dropped as I saw a pack of enormous werewolves, including Stewart, who gave me a look of desperate werewolf longing before he turned away and resumed forlornly licking his private parts. As I watched, saddened and guilt-ridden because of the pain I had inflicted on him by being so attractive without making any conscious effort, I saw more shapes emerge from a third side of the clearing. This time it was Denise's jaw that dropped, as it fell from Phil's hand when he saw who it was:

His vampire family: Grover, Buck, Scooter, Eldridge, DeeDee, Trixie, and Skeeter. Despite the obvious seriousness of the situation, there was no mistaking how good-looking they all were. Grover nodded to Phil with a special code vampire nod, indicating something ominous was about to transpire.

"Stay here," asserted Phil, flinging aside what I think was Denise's thorax. "Stay perfectly still. Whatever you do, *don't do anything to draw attention to yourself.*"

I wanted to shout something that would stop Phil, such as "Stop, Phil!" But he had already become a blur of speed like a really chiseled supernatural Road Runner as he raced toward the middle of the clearing, where an incredible battle had erupted between the werewolves and the various attractive sets of vampires. There were snarls and roars and hideous supernatural screams as the fighting raged at fantastic speeds all around me. It was incredibly exciting and terrifying, although because of my trademark inability to describe action in anything except very general terms you are just going to have to take my word for this.

It was all happening so fast that I couldn't tell who was winning and who was losing. But as the battle raged on, an alarming thought crept into my mind: *I was not playing a central role.* I realized that I needed to do something. But what could I, a mere human, although a highly endearing one, do? Then it struck me: *I could draw attention to myself.*

Frantically I looked around, searching for a sharp object. Suddenly I saw it, lying on the ground, clearly visible in the bright moonlight:

A sharp object.

I picked it up and stabbed at myself. I was aiming for my arm, but because of my trademark clumsiness I actually stabbed one of Denise's arms, a piece of which broke off and flew into my right leg, leaving a deep gash. Blood streamed redly down my leg. Suddenly there was a vampire stampede coming my way at the speed of vampire, with the werewolves right behind. The vampires came from all directions, their fangs extended to the length of No. 3 Phillips screwdrivers.

In the crowd I caught sight of Phil, who had a look of deep horrified concern on his face, and even in that moment, knowing I was definitely going to die in seconds although obviously I didn't because here I am narrating this, I remember thinking how good-looking he was, and wondering how he got his hair to always stay at exactly that level of tousle.

Now they were almost on me, dozens of blood-crazed vampires and enraged werewolves. I knew there was no way I could be saved. I heard Phil shout, "No!" Then I heard a howl of despair from Stewart. Then, in the distance, I heard the distinctive hydraulic sound of an anguished Zamboni.

And then, at the absolute climactic height of the action sequence, everything went dark.

CHAPTER FOUR

Resolution

"She's coming around," I heard Phil's voice intone. Raising my eyelids, I opened my eyes. I was lying on my back, and a small piece of Denise's back. Hovering above me were Phil, Stewart, and Sven, as well as Phil's family, and the Jonas Brothers.

"What happened?" I queried weakly.

Phil shook his head lovingly. "You almost got yourself

and all of us killed because of your unbelievably irrespon-
sible, deranged, and self-centered behavior," he remarked,
adding, "but that just makes me desire you more, you
crazy, quirky, irresistible woman, you."

Stewart and Sven moved their heads vertically up and
down in nods of agreement.

"But how did you win the climactic fight?" I pressed.

"Through a lot of action," Phil explained.

"Wow," I stated. "It must have been incredibly exciting."

"It was," he concurred with a twinkle in his tawny eyes.

"But what are the Jonas Brothers doing here?" I persisted.

"We love you," they stated in unison.

"Join the club," I sighed in rueful resignation, drawing
hearty supernatural chuckles all around. "Well," I went on,
"at least our other troubles are over."

Phil looked at me with an expression of not totally
agreeing with my assertion.

"What is it?" I interrogated, adding, "Is something wrong?"

"The Gambinis are very upset," he replied pensively.
"They vowed to return with a huge vampire army and kill
everybody in the Pacific Northwest, including Boise."

I nodded, struck once again by the way Phil's gorgeous
cheekbones accented the chiseled perfection of his chin.

"Also," he went on, "it turns out that all those recent
hiker deaths were not caused by Denise, but by a long-
dormant supernatural race of giant homicidal pine cones

who have been awakened by global warming and now prowl the woods around Creepstone each night, savagely attacking every living thing in their path."

"I thought that was just a Native American legend," I protested, fighting the urge to run my hand through the tousled perfection of Phil's hair.

"If only," he muttered. "It's only a matter of time before they come into town and are attracted to you. And on top of all that, there's also the fact that Stewart and I are still mortal enemies who could very well kill each other in our relentless struggle to possess you."

"Don't forget about me," chimed in Sven.

"And us," assented the Jonas Brothers.

"Me too!" called a voice from a distance.

"Who was that?" I inquired.

"Zac Efron," observed Phil.

Oh no, I reflected.

"I love you!" shouted Zac Efron, getting closer. "I want to—"

His voice was suddenly cut off. I heard a harsh chomping sound.

"What happened?" I ventured.

"Pine cone got him," responded Stewart. "Those things are *fast*."

"We'd better get back to town," suggested Phil warily.

"Yes," I assented eagerly. Pete would be regaining consciousness soon.

Phil picked me up in his gorgeous sculpted arms and began running with impossible swiftness through the trees toward Creepstone, followed by Stewart and Sven, and, much farther behind, by the Jonas Brothers, who lack supernatural speed but are very cute. Reflecting in my mind on how much I had made all of these males suffer, I vowed mentally to stop, once and for all, being such an indecisive, self-centered ninny.

Until the next book.

A Festival of
Grimness

'm standing next to a soccer field at the Wide World of Sports complex in Walt Disney World, the Happiest Place on Earth. There are two men standing about twenty feet from me. They are not happy. Their faces are the color of wild cherry cough drops, and they are shouting.

"GET IT OUT OF THERE!" one of them shouts.

"GET IT OUT!" the other one affirms, adding, by way of explanation, "GET IT OUT! GET IT OUT! GET IT OUT!!"

The men are shouting at nine-year-old girls, presumably their daughters, playing in a big soccer tournament. The girls are trying to kick a ball away from their goal. The men are not satisfied with their efforts.

"*GET IT OUT OF THERE!!!*" shouts the first one, so violently that I half-expect him to expel a chunk of trachea onto the perfect Disney grass. But the man doesn't attract any attention, because there are hundreds of other adults around, watching dozens of games, most of them shouting just as loud, and sounding just as unhappy. If you didn't know any better, you'd think all these people were furious at their children.

But of course they're not: They're modern American parents raising modern American children, and God forbid that a modern American child should engage in an athletic activity without being shouted at by adults.

"GET! IT! OUT! OF! THERE!" shouts one of the sideline dads, who is now so worked up that his words are coming out in bold-faced type.

The other dad, sensing a teachable moment, shouts, "KIMBERLY! *WHAT ARE YOU DOING???*"

When I was a child, things were different. For one thing, North America was covered by glaciers. For another thing, when it came to sports, we kids were pretty much on our own. Where I lived, in Armonk, N.Y., the only organized sport was Little League, and aside from the dads who coached the teams, there were few grown-ups around. When the games were going on, my dad was on the train home from another long day in New York City, wearing a hat, smoking, and reading the newspaper in a car full of other smoking, hat-wearing, paper-reading dads. My mom had four kids to manage, so the last thing she had time for was to sit in the bleachers at the Wampus[1] School ball field and watch me scurry around right field like a disoriented gerbil in a desperate and almost always futile effort to position myself where the ball was going to come down.

So Little League was really just for us kids. We rode our bikes to the field, played the game, and rode our bikes home. At dinner our parents might ask us how the game went, but they might not. It was not a big deal either way. We didn't expect the grown-ups to think it was all that important. *We* didn't think it was all that important. It was *Little League*. If an adult had appeared at the Wampus ball field and spent an entire game yelling at the players, everybody would have thought that person was a lunatic.

The other sports we played had no adult involvement whatsoever—no coaches, no referees, no league officials, no scorekeepers, no uniforms. We played anywhere we could, including living rooms, with whoever was around—three on a side, nineteen on a side, one on a side, whatever. We picked our own teams and made our own rules and argued a lot and played until it was so dark that while trying to catch a football that you could not see you might (this happened to me) run face-first into a tree that you also could not see.

Nobody watched us play these sports. Nobody encouraged us from the sideline. But we managed to have fun anyway. And we

---

1. Yes, "Wampus."

went on to become a strong and proud generation that survived the Great Depression and won World War II.

No, wait, that was my parents' generation. My generation's big achievements ran more along the lines of spending junior year abroad. But we did learn some important life lessons from sports. I learned, for example, that even though I was not as big, or fast, or strong, or coordinated as the other kids, if I worked really hard—if I gave 100 percent and never quit—I would still be smaller, slower, weaker, and less coordinated than the other kids. In other words, I learned that even though I enjoyed playing sports, I sucked at them. And understanding that you suck at some things is useful information in life. The world would be a better place if people were fully cognizant of their areas of suckage.

For example: I have, over the years, received in the mail approximately 17 million manuscripts from people whose goal is to become professional writers. They want me to discover them, encourage them, mentor them, find them an agent, etc. Some of these people have talent; some have actually become professional writers. But a great many of them will never become professional writers, because—follow me closely here—they are not good at writing. Of course I don't *tell* them that. Probably nobody will ever tell them that. They will continue to try and fail, and in the end they'll be bitter, like the early-round contestants on *American Idol* who think they got booted because Simon

Cowell is mean, rather than because their singing sounds like a bull being castrated with a hockey stick.

These contestants humiliated themselves on national TV because when they were growing up, loving to sing, always singing around the house, no thoughtful family member or caring friend ever had the kindness to put a hand on their shoulder and say, in a gentle and loving voice, "You suck." They needed Simon Cowells, but instead they were surrounded by Randy Jacksons and Paula Abduls, trying to be nice, not wanting to hurt their feelings, and thus setting them up for failure. Because the cruel fact is that the world does not reward suckage, outside of Washington, D.C.

Take nature. If you are a wildebeest that happens to be bad at running fast, you will fail. You might have a sincere *desire* to run fast, and you might *believe* you can run fast, because when you're hanging out at the water hole, other wildebeests—the Randy and Paula wildebeests—are telling you what you want to hear: *Sure, dog! You run pretty fast!* But when the cheetah shows up and the herd takes off, you will be a wildeburger. You would have been much better off if you had accepted your limitations and gone into some other line of endeavor more suited to your talents, such as sloth, or professional writer.

Speaking of which:

Beep! Beep! Beep!

That's the sound of what we writing professionals call the

Segue Warning Horn, telling our readers to hold on tight as we make a sharp turn and attempt to get back to our original topic, which you may recall is youth sports.

Here's the problem: A lot of parents are insane. You may be one of these parents without even knowing it, because the craziness takes you over gradually.

It's not a problem when your child is really little. My daughter started playing soccer when she was four; at that stage, the parents have no choice but to be mellow. You can't take the games seriously, because four-year-olds are unaware of many key elements of soccer. The ball, for example. The players may notice it on occasion, but they don't feel the need to become personally *involved* with it. They have other things on their minds. They'll see one of their friends, and they'll think, "Hey! There's Stella! I'll give her a hug!" Also at any random moment they might feel the need to lie down, or skip off the field, or do a cartwheel, or get some nose-picking done. What with one thing and another, they don't have a lot of time to devote to the ball.

So at this stage your role, as a parent, is to watch for those rare moments when your child and the ball are in the same general vicinity, and then shout: "Kick the ball!" And then, on the off chance that your child does kick the ball, you shout: "No! The other way!" That's it. You do that for maybe forty minutes, during which time either (a) nobody scores, or (b) both teams score eighty-seven times, and then it's time for cupcakes.

So in the beginning the soccer parents are fairly relaxed. But pretty soon the kids start to get the hang of the sport. The games become more competitive; score is kept; league standings are published. There are no more cartwheels.

This is when some parents start to change. They shout more, and their shouting takes on an urgent, even angry, tone. They shout at the officials, and sometimes at the coaches, but above all they shout at the kids. These parents will *tell* you that sports are about having fun, but they clearly are not having fun, especially when they—excuse me, I mean when their *kids*—lose. Again, not all parents act like this. But a lot of them do, and they're the ones who tend to dominate the sideline mood, which becomes more and more serious.

The parents of my daughter's team have, so far, managed to resist this trend. We've been together for five years, and we're still fairly mellow on the sideline, unless you count my wife, who is both Cuban and Jewish and therefore genetically programmed to produce more words in any given hour, awake or asleep, than the entire state of Wyoming. But hers are generally words of encouragement, such as "Good try!" and "You can do it!" and (to our daughter) "Stop fiddling with your hair!"

The rest of us parents watch the game and cheer as needed, but we're also chatting, reading, texting, and occasionally, during evening games, sneaking snorts of adult beverages that some thoughtful parent has snuck in along with the snacks. We view games at least partly as pleasant social events. Our daughters do, too.

We were not prepared for the Disney World tournament. We began to realize what we'd gotten into when, in our first game, the opposing team showed up with a large, professionally made team banner on a pole at least ten feet long, which two of the fathers planted in the turf. That's right: a *banner*. It would not surprise me if, for home games, they also had a blimp.

Another intimidating factor was that the opposing girls were larger than our girls. I'm pretty sure some of them were wearing brassieres. They went through an elaborate warm-up routine, and at various points did these coordinated military-sounding cheers, like small brassiere-wearing Navy SEALS. When the game started, the opposing parents—most of whom were wearing team colors—shouted intensely the entire time.

They killed us. And the thing was, the more goals they scored, the more intensely the parents shouted. It was as if they wanted their girls to *destroy* our girls. I will admit that I developed a strong dislike toward those parents. I wanted to go over and tell them to shut up. But I didn't, for fear they would impale me with their banner pole.

We played two more games in the tournament before we were, mercifully, eliminated. We got creamed in both of them, scoring a total of zero goals. In one of the games, when our girls had fallen far behind and clearly were going to lose badly, the opposing parents, who were wearing matching team T-shirts, started an organized chant calling for *more goals*.

And these were parents of nine-year-olds. The parents of the older teams were even more intense. Everywhere you went at the tournament you saw people staring unhappily at the field and barking instructions at their kids. Occasionally, when a team scored, there would be a brief outburst of joy from the parents of that team, and reactions of disgust from the opposing parents. Then everybody would resume staring and barking. The air was thick with parental pressure. It was a festival of grimness.

You might be thinking: "You're just being critical because your team got its butt kicked." There may be some truth to that. Maybe if our girls had won, I'd have loved the tournament. Maybe I'd have bought a professional banner.

But I don't think so. I think that no matter what happened, I'd have found the tournament to be kind of depressing. I think that parents—not all of them, but a lot of them—are sucking the fun out of kids' sports. They're making it clear to their kids that they think sports is about winning, and *only* winning. This is a reasonable value to instill if you honestly believe your child is going to become a professional athlete. But you need to remember two things:

1. Your child is not, in fact, going to become a professional athlete.
2. There are more important things in life than winning. Such as not being a jerk.

Your kids don't need you shouting at them on the playing field, any more than they need you shouting at them in the classroom. Let them play the game and figure out for themselves how they feel about it, without having to worry about your feelings, too. Make it clear that your happiness doesn't depend on the score. Cheer for your kid, sure, but do it *cheerfully*. If you can't manage that, take a walk; the game will go on fine without you, because it's not about you.

And if, while you're taking your walk, you happen to pass a girls' soccer game, and you notice a group of parents who are sitting and chatting in a relaxed manner except for one Cuban-Jewish woman who is so animated that calming her down would require tranquilizer darts, stop and say hi. Maybe we can offer you a refreshing snuck-in adult beverage. Because you are, after all, an adult.

Right?

Father of
the Groom

On my son's wedding day, when I saw him standing up there in front of everybody, waiting for his bride, I had this sudden, intense awareness of the passage of time. To me, it seemed as if only a few days had passed since Rob was playing happily in my living room, flying his remote-control helicopter.

Then I realized that in fact only a few days *had* passed. I got him the remote-control helicopter as his wedding gift. He may be a grown man, but he's still a guy.

Anyway, it was an amazing feeling, watching my son get married. The whole weekend was very emotional for me; I cried like a baby. And that was just when I saw the bill for the rehearsal dinner.[1]

---

1. Rim shot.

But seriously, before I say anything that might be construed as a criticism of the vast and constantly expanding wedding-industrial complex, which currently accounts for 38 percent of the U.S. economy, let me state for the record that I *loved* my son's wedding. He found a wonderful bride in Laura—a smart, beautiful, warm, talented, and funny woman who is absolutely perfect for him. They had the best wedding in human history, and I am not saying this solely because I had many glasses of champagne and danced with approximately twenty-seven women *simultaneously* to "Play That Funky Music, White Boy."

So I have no complaints about the wedding. I must say, however, that the *planning* of the wedding was a tad stressful, in the same sense that the universe is a tad spacious. And for good reason: Planning a modern wedding is comparable in scope to constructing a nuclear power plant, although the wedding is more complex because—to pick just one of many examples—a nuclear power plant does not require floral installations. These used to be called "flowers," but that was before the florists—excuse me, I mean the floral-installation artists—realized that "floral installations" is more professional, as measured by how much you can charge for installing them.

Which brings us to budgeting. Here's my advice for parents who are going to be planning a wedding: At the very beginning, decide exactly how much money is the *absolute maximum* you are willing to spend. Write this number down on a piece of paper and *keep it with you at all times.* That way, when the wedding is over, you can pull it out, look at the number, and laugh until a streamer of drool reaches all the way down to your feet, which will be bare inasmuch as you can no longer afford shoes.

Here's the problem. The bridal magazines, which depend for their existence on advertisements for the wedding-industrial complex, have for decades been hammering home the three core principles of the modern American wedding:

FIRST PRINCIPLE: Your wedding is the most important day of your life, so you want it to be perfect.

SECOND PRINCIPLE: However, it does not have to cost a lot of money.

THIRD PRINCIPLE: However, if it doesn't, it will suck.

These principles resonate powerfully with your modern bride-to-be, because ever since she was a little girl she has been fantasizing about her wedding day. This is not true of your modern groom-to-be. When he was a little boy, he was—I state this with authority—conducting experiments to see what happens when you set fire to He-Man action figures.[2]

But the bride has been dreaming for years about having a fairy-tale wedding, patterned after the wedding scene in the Walt Disney animated film *Cinderella*, wherein Cinderella and

2. What happens is, they get *even more hideous*.

Prince Charming ride off into the sunset in a horse-drawn carriage while the cute little mice wave goodbye. What they *don't* show you in this film is parents in bare feet paying the bills for the carriage rental, the horse supplier, the mouse wrangler, the sunset-installation professional, etc. Because all of these things cost money. And if you hold the wedding in New York City, as we did, all of these things will cost *extra* money, because you will be paying for *unionized* mouse wranglers.

True Story: My wife inquired, at the hotel where we held the rehearsal dinner, about the cost of renting a projector and screen so we could show pictures of Rob and Laura as guests arrived. The hotel said that, counting the fee for the two workers[3] required, by union contract, to set the equipment up, it would cost us—I am not making this up—*eighteen hundred dollars*. Which of course is more than it would cost, outside of Planet Manhattan, to *buy* a projector and screen, as well as a used car to drive them home in.

My point is that putting on a modern wedding is an expensive and complicated undertaking, which is why many people these days hire a professional wedding planner, whose function is to make it even *more* expensive and complicated. The planner works closely with the bride, as well as the only other really es-

---

3. No, I don't know why it would require two workers. Maybe there's a screen union, and a projector union. Or maybe there are different unions for plugging and unplugging.

sential person in the wedding, by which I of course mean the bride's mother.

At this point the groom is pretty much out of the picture. If the wedding were a solar system, the bride would be the sun; her mom would be another, slightly smaller nearby sun; the wedding planner would be a third sun; the caterer, floral installation professional, photographer, videographer, cake design engineer, etc., would be planets orbiting these suns; and the groom would be an asteroid the size of a regulation softball 73 trillion light-years away. Sometimes the groom gets so far out of the wedding-planning loop that the planners forget to invite him to the actual wedding and the bride, at the last minute, has to marry a member of the catering staff. (This happened to Madonna *twice*.)

Fortunately Rob made it to his wedding, and, as I say, it was a grand day. Rob looked handsome and nervous; Laura looked radiant; they both looked beyond happy. For me, the highlight of the service was the exchange of vows, which was performed by six union vow-exchangers.

No, seriously, Rob and Laura wrote and spoke their own vows. Hers were funny and smart and sweet, and Rob's—I say with a father's pride—were amazing. When he told her, with pure and simple eloquence, how much he loved her, his voice broke, and every woman watching went *aww*, and Laura's eyes shone like moonlight on a mountain lake. And if you could watch that—your son, the boy you used to carry on your shoulders and tuck in at night, now a grown man putting his heart out there in front of everybody for the woman he adores—if you could watch that and not spill tears all over your tuxedo dress shirt, then you'd be missing out on the one thing that made all the wedding hassle worthwhile. I'm talking about the champagne.

No, I'm talking about the love between Rob and Laura. It radiated from them and filled the room, infusing all of us with joy. It was a feeling that lingered even after the reception ended and we rode back to the hotel in a taxi driven by a man who spent the whole trip carrying on a loud cell-phone conversation in what I believe was Martian; I even felt a certain affection toward *him*.

OK, that was the champagne.